FOREWORD

This century has witnessed four peak offensives of black workers' struggles in South Africa, each involving 50,000 and
150,000 unionized workers. The first three were broken as a
result of state repression and internal organizational weakness on the part of the trade unions. The fourth offensive
still continues . The focus of this research report is this
recent rise in workers' organization and militancy since the
early 1970's and the state's reaction to these developments. The
report is up to date as of early autumn 1981.

The black workers' trade union organization and mass strikes
have forcefully demonstrated the intensified political and
economic contradictions ins the past decade. The critical importance of black workers' struggles to real and meaningful
change in South Africa thus warrants a thorough study if their
nature, scope and potential impact in the liberation struggle
in southern Africa and abroad.

I sincerely thank all friends and colleagues, and contacts in
the black workers' struggle; also the Centre for Development
Research in Copenhagen and the Scandinavian Institute of African Studies in Uppsala for having made fact-finding, writing
and the publishing of this report possible.

Maputo in November 1982
Jens Haarløv

CONTENTS

1. INTRODUCTION

South Africa at the beginning of the 1980's is one of the countries in the world where the sharpest contradictions between different social groups are found. Throughout this century the country has been characterized by a form of state which excluded the black majority from any influence on the development of society. The blacks have been forced to accept a role as unskilled labourers in the mines, farms and manufacturing industry. Protests against the existing system have usually been met with brutal repression.

However, since the beginning of the 1970's it has been more and more evident that the stability of the system is severely threatened. The reason for this is the economic and political crises in the country. The economic crisis consists mainly in the lack of skilled workers and the economy's continued dependence on the farming and mining sectors. Politically the crisis is shown by the ever in-creasing resistance to the present system. The resistance can take many forms; for example illegal armed struggle, community-organization, school-boycotts and trade union organization.

The government's reply to the crisis has taken two forms. Firstly, an intensification of repression and an insistence on maintaining key features of the apartheid system; for example the migrant worker system and the denial of demo-cratic rights to blacks. Secondly, the government has carried out certain reforms; for example the abolition of parts of so-called "petty-apartheid" and an extension of the rights to seek jobs in an urban area for the blacks who live there permanently.

Within this very broad framework I have chosen to focus on one aspect of the political crisis: the black workers' struggle in the form of mass strikes and trade union organization, and on one of the main areas in which reforms have been carried out: labour market regulation.

Thus, it is important to bear in mind that the following analysis does not try to cover the total political and economic situation. This does not mean that these aspects are ignored. On the contrary, they form the basis of the analysis. But if they should have been included systematically, only very limited space would have been left for the real topic of the analysis.[1]

I will stress three reasons why analysis of labour struggles and the labour market is important. Firstly, it leads us to the core of the apartheid system: the extreme exploitation and control of the black labour force. Their attempts to improve their wage and working conditions through organized labour movements, in order to back up their demands for political and social changes, and the government's efforts to pacify the black workers by introducing reforms in the regulation of the labour market, are therefore crucial for understanding the future prospects of the apartheid system.

Secondly, the black workers have a potentially powerful position in the South African economy. They constitute approximately 70 % of the labour force, and could, given the right conditions, paralyse most economic activities in the country. Analysing the process of change in South Africa it is therefore essential to evaluate the black workers' actual position of strength and the political line they pursue.

The third reason why the black labour struggle in South Africa is important is the influence it will have on the future shape and form of South African politics. The working class in South Africa is very large in comparison to other African countries. A study of the political line of the South African working class can reveal important clues of the future role they will play both nationally and continentally in the post-liberation period.

The central issue in this report is to determine whether the state has re-adjusted its labour relation policies in the period since 1970 and if so, to determine the character of these changes and to analyse the strategies employed by the black workers.

In regard to state policy an analysis will attempt to determine, firstly, whether the state still uses its physical power as the only means of containing the black workers' struggle, and whether the changes in labour market policy since 1970 are purely formal or represent a significant shift in state policy.

The following analysis of state policy is geared around three policy options. A repressive policy involves the denial of union rights for black workers and an attempt to crush existing black trade unions. A co-optive policy attempts to absorb union leaders in the institutions of the dominant classes, whereby they are given a platform, but without an independent power base. The position of the black workers in society is therefore not strengthened. A democratization policy, as distinct from a co-optive policy, permits independent unions with their own power base in workers' organization at the factory floor. Such trade unions are able to have an independent political voice, and their existence strengthens the relative power position of the dominated classes in society.

In this context, it is important to analyse the politics of the black labour movement. How will black workers react to a policy of continued repression: Will the black workers and trade unions settle for reforms which will to some extent allow them some concessions, for example, wage negotiations, but at the cost of their independence?

The politics of the trade union movement is best analysed in terms of three dimensions:

- reformist contra revolutionary struggle.

- mass strikes and spontaneous action contra an organized trade union struggle.

- legal contra illegal struggle.

For example, in order to measure the effectiveness of a co-optive policy in stabilizing the situation it is essential to know whether a revolutionary struggle is predominant among the black workers. This in turn is closely related to the different perspectives and possibilities of a legal or an illegal movement and whether these are contradictory or complementary. Mass strikes seem to be a very strong and effective weapon of the black trade unions. How has this particular strategy been used, and with what results?

My preliminary hypothesis is that there has actually been a shift in state policy in the 1970's. The offensive actions of the black workers forced the state to supplement its repressive policy with some co-optive initiatives.

However, it should be emphasized that it is highly improbable that the black workers will accept a co-optive model. The contention here is that the apartheid-system as such furthers a tendency among the black workers to develop revolutionary consciousness.

The basis for this postulate is:

- that the state's constant involvement in labour struggles in favour of the employers indicates that the black workers' struggle against the employers can rather easily be changed into a fight against the existing state structures,

- that the political and legal discrimination against blacks block any tendency of the black workers to conceive of themselves as isolated individuals in society. The political and legal system contributes to the political awareness of the black workers in that they conceive themselves more and more as a class with common interests,

- that there has never existed a reformist tradition among the black workers, because there has never really been a continuous improvement in the living conditions of the black workers in the history of the Republic.

In addition, totalitarian systems face severe problems when they attempt reforms. They make the attempts precisely because they can no longer control the dominated classes' struggle against the existing system, but at the same time the totalitarian systems must put severe limitations to reforms because a total democratization would trigger colossal forces for change. Hence the reforms initiated by a totalitarian regime are likely to be very limited. This also implies that the demands of the dominated classes can not be satisfied, and the final result will be a further intensification of the social struggle. In our specific context this implies[2] that the changes in labour regulation introduced by the South African state will not be likely to succeed in directing the revolutionary struggle of the black workers.

This research report consists of four main section. The first section will be concerned with mass strikes, the second with the black trade unions, and the third with the legal framework for regulating the labour market. The final section consists of a summary and survey of future prospects.

A note on terminology. 'Black trade unions' or 'Black workers struggle' refer primarily to the predominant African trade unions or African workers' activities. But the terms also include coloured or Indian unions and workers that side with the blacks. Furthermore most of the 'black' unions are non-racial and might therefore have some members who are not Africans.

Notes

1 In my final thesis in political science, which was written together with Søren Schmidt (see literature list), we tried to cover the total political and economic situation, but we had also four times as many pages as this Research Report has.

2 In spite of the formal democracy for whites I think it is justified to talk about South Africa as a totalitarian state. Especially in the light of the recent attempts to centralize power around the Prime Minister and the increasing influence of the military over the decision-making process.

2. MASS STRIKES

2.1 INTRODUCTION

An analysis of mass strikes requires some preliminary dis-
tinctions. Firstly, one can distinguish between demonstra-
tive. strikes which are normally relatively short-term and
are primarily a method of a showing the unity and strength
of the workers, and the more long-term trials of strength,
where the respective parties' perseverance is decisive for
the outcome.[1] Secondly, one can distinguish between spontaneous mass strikes and mass strikes that are relatively
organized. Thirdly, it can be very useful to distinguish
between mass strikes on the basis of the demands being
made. Mass strikes can be started in order to carry through;
- isolated economic demands,
- purely political demands,
- both economic and political demands.

The relation between the economic and political content of
mass strikes is an important theme in the history of the
revolutionary socialist movement. Rosa Luxemburg pointed
out how a spontaneous mass strike can often raise the level
of class awareness, and is usually transformed to smaller
strikes that focus on economic demands. Lenin pointed out
the importance of the degree of organization behind a
mass strike, and how a mass strike gradually becomes rad-
icalized and how the economic demands became intertwined
with political demands. Both Luxemburg and Lenin emphasize,
although from different premises, the dynamic interplay
between economic and political demands.[2]

Finally, I will stress the importance of Sartre's contribu-
tion to an understanding of what a mass strike can mean to
the dominated classes' self-awareness and practice. Sartre
describes how social groups whose members normally function
in isolation, are hereby able to recognize their common
interests and transform them into action.[3]

2.2 THE DURBAN STRIKES OF 1973

The social background to the Durban strikes must be seen in
the light of three factors.[4] Firstly, the increasing importance for the economy of black manpower. During the economic
boom in 1960's the number of black workers engaged in waged

labour doubled, but without improvements in wages and working conditions.

Secondly, the situation became even more aggravated at the beginning of the 1970's due to an explosive rise in prices which resulted in a drastic fall in real wages, while the white bourgeoisie and its allies within the white population experienced an impressive rise in their standard of living.[5]

Thirdly, the importance of the militant strikes that took place in South Africa & Namibia from 1970-72 should be stressed. The strikes involved contract-workers in Namibia, dock workers in Durban, and bus drivers in Johannesburg. The contract-workers' strike in Namibia was clearly the most comprehensive protest, with over 13,500 workers who stopped work, and even though only a few of their demands were fulfilled, the workers nevertheless attained a 60-100 % wage increase.

An investigation in 1971-72 studied the black workers conception of their own situation.[6] The investigations revealed the existence of a widespread dissatisfaction with the current situation, coupled with awareness of the need for collective action. A nucleus of workers were politically aware and capable of attracting many workers to participate in an eventual action or strike - even many of the 40 % who did not believe that their hopeless situation could be changed.

The Durban strikes took place in January and February 1973 and can be divided into three phases:
1) A series of diffuse and scattered strikes from the 9th to the 25th of January.
2) A massive wave of strikes in the whole of the Durban area, which lasted until the 9th of February, and,
3) A rapid decline in the mass strike from the 9th to the 15th of February.

However, there were many scattered strikes in the latter part of February and March. As Luxemburg pointed out, a strike of the masses is often transformed into many smaller strikes based on wage demands.

Within these three phases, I should first point out that the strikes began at a relatively large factory. It received much coverage in the press, and relatively quickly the striking workers attained a significant raise in wages. During the second period the strikers mainly consisted of textile and municipal workers. A total of 16,000 municipal workers went on strike, including many Indians. The second phase of the strike involved well over 50,000 people from approximately 100 factories. When the textile and municipal workers were offered nearly a 20 % raise in salary on the 7th of February they accepted this relatively quickly. During the third phase it was remarkable that only a few of the workers on strike (0.2 %) were prosecuted by the authorities, in spite of the fact that the strikes were illegal. On the whole there were few cases of direct physical intervention from the ever-present police and the military.

The first question that arises is why the strikes began in Durban and, as we have seen, spread so rapidly within the industrial area of Durban.

It is essential to point out here that in 1973 South Africa's largest concentration of manufacturing industries was located in the Durban-Pinetown region, and that the factories are placed very close to each other. This has meant that if workers go on strike in one factory the news will spread very quickly, and if, as it happened in this particular case, the workers march on Durban City, the process becomes even more rapid.

Another reason why the strikes achieved the proportions that they did was the fact that the striking textile workers were all employed by the same concern - The Frame group - known for its low wages and poor working conditions. The fact that the municipal workers had a single employer could also have contributed to the rapid spread of the strike.

In the terms of the introductory discussion about mass strikes it is obvious that the Durban strikes were demonstrations rather than a long term trial of strength. For example, the 16,000 municipal workers' strike lasted only a few days, and the textile workers strike, the longest, lasted a little over 10 days.

As regards the organized and more spontaneous element of strikes they were essentially spontaneous in the sense that they did not have a central leadership to coordinate and determine the timing of the strike and the demands being raised, to bargain with the employers etc. This is not to say, however, that there was a total lack of organisation. On the contrary, the character of mass strikes:

"Depends on the preexistence of informal communication networks, and these must include informal organization within the factories."[7]

The spontaneity was on the one hand a weakness because it involved lack of co-ordination etc, but on the other hand it was a force to be reckoned with, because the very effective security police could not paralyse the strikes by locking up the leadership. The absence of overall coordination strengthened the organization at the grassroot level. Informal decision- and communication networks were used and new ones created.

This had a strong influence on the growth of the organized trade union struggle in the 1970's.

In regard to the political and economic content of the strikes the workers initially demanded a doubling or trippling of wage rates.[8]

The point here is that even though the Durban strikes were primarily a struggle for better wages, the size of the wage demands and the character of the strikes as a whole gave them a political dimension. The workers' demand for a raise in their wages ranging from two to three times that of their present wage was clearly not possible within the framework of South Africa's political structure. The low wage level is the very nucleus of the apartheid system. Therefore, the very high wage-demands by the workers became a political manifestation against a system which could not offer a satisfactory standard of living. The strikes were also, ipso facto, a political act. According to the Bantu Labour (settlement of Disputes) Act of 1953 the strikes were illegal, and the works committees, which the law intended to establish, failed to function according to plan. There were only 24 works committees in all. The system's lack of ability to stem the black workers' demands was clearly demonstrated. The strikes therefore indirectly represented a political demand to the government about revising the existing regulation of the labour market.

In summarizing the evaluation of the Durban strikes, I
would emphasize that they are a good illustration of
Sartre's thesis of how the mass strike can lead to increased
collective action.

The Durban strikes became the event which marked the end of
the black workers' defensive struggle, which had lasted for
over a decade. In chapter two I will return to the trade
union organization that the strikes gave rise to. Here I
will continue with the Soweto strikes. Like the Durban
strikes they were mass strikes, but nevertheless there
are several important differences between the two.

2.3 THE SOWETO-STRIKES OF 1976

On June 16th, 1976 heavily armed police opened fire on
black school children who were peacefully demonstrating
against the introduction of Afrikaans as the official language in the schools. This was the beginning of one of the
most widespread confrontations between the dominant and the
dominated classes in South Africa. The protests against
Afrikaans was the spark that ignited a wave of protest
throughout the country against the apartheid system.

As to the background for what is generally known as the
uprising in Soweto, I will highlight two aspects. Firstly,
the Nationalist Party's attempt to eliminate the dominance
of the English language and culture, and to replace this
with the Afrikaans language and moral code. Secondly, the
resistance to this move, especially among the black youths
due to the blacks' growing awareness of their own strength,
values and rights.

I will not present a more thorough analysis of the course
of events that took place in the summer of 1976 with the
burning of public buildings, police brutality etc. The reader
is referred to other works. Instead I concentrate on the
three mass strikes that followed in the wake of the Soweto
uprising during the 1st and 3rd week of August, and in the
middle of September.

The first strike took place on the 4th of August with
approximately 60 % of Johannesburg's black workers taking
part.

The initiative came from the black students, and in order to carry it through physical intimidation was used to prevent workers from entering their workplace, rather than agitating and convincing them that the strike was a justified one. Train stations were blockaded, busses stopped and even railtracks were damaged.[10] This type of action created some tension between the young and some of the workers; among others some migrant labourers, tension the police were not slow to exploit during the next strike.

It took only approximately 10 days for the students to realize their mistake and revise their strategy. Now the students sought to activate the workers through dialogue and conviction. The Soweto Student Representative Council (SSRC) stated that the students had advanced so far as they could by protesting, and that it was now essential that the industrial workers used their power-base in the economy.

The initiative for the second strike did not come from the students, but from the illegal liberation-movement , the ANC.[12] In pamphlets the ANC encouraged the workers to go on a three-day strike from the 23rd to the 25th of August. The employers reported an absentee rate of about 75-80 % among their employees, and in some places the figures were as high as 90-98 % of the workforce. The majority of the participants were among the unskilled and organized workers. On the second day of the strike the police succeeded in splitting the ranks of the black workers. The erroneous tactics of the students during the first strike was now being used to set up a group of migrant workers against the strikers and the students. Hundreds of Zulu migrant workers from the myriad of tribal 'hostels' for single men marched angrily in protest through Soweto. On the 8th of August 21 people were killed and 197 wounded as a result of the migrant workers' assault. It was reported that heavily armed police quietly watched while the black workers fought against each other, or directly encouraged the Zulu workers to further violence.[13] However, among other things an intervention by the Kwa-zulu bantustan leader G. Buthelezi reduced the tension between the resident-workers and the migrants, and in September during the mass strike the migrant workers were out in full support.

The strikes that took place from the 13th to the 15th of September became the most comprehensive of the mass strikes in 1976. This time the strikes spread from the Johannesburg area to Cape Town, where hundreds of thousands of African and coloured workers went on strike. In all over half a million workers took part in the strikes. This time the strikes were better prepared, more disciplined and more unified than earlier: There were, for example, no reports of the use of violence by the strikers. SSRC had called the strike and it should be viewed as a general protest against the system of Apartheid as such, and the repression the blacks had been exposed to during the previous months. There were no common concrete economic or short-term political demands during the strikes. In Cape Town leaflets were distributed urging the workers to strike on economic grounds, while others concentrated on the abolishment of racial discrimination. There were no concrete demands made during the earlier strikes either. For example, there were no wage demands, demands for improvements in Soweto (for example, electricity), demands for political changes in Soweto's administration, or in any other specifically defined region such as trade union rights and the abolishment of the Bantustan citizenship. The mass strikes were general protests against the system.

The dynamic interplay between the economic and political demands, which Lenin and Luxemburg perceived as an ideal form for an effective mass strike did not occur during the Soweto strikes. This weakens the foundation and strength of the strikes, and impedes the recruitment of new workers.

There is a risk that such strikes will exhaust and demoralise the workers because their very broad political and economic demands usually do not result in any concrete changes. An indirect proof of this came when the SSRC urged the workers to strike once again from 1st to the 11th of November. Only a few workers supported the strike.[14]

Compared with the different types of mass strikes, the Soweto strikes were clearly <u>political demonstrations</u>. This distinguishes the Soweto from the Durban strikes where the economic demands were most prominent. Another difference in relation to the Durban strikes is that there was a centralized initiative and timing behind the Soweto strikes.

However, the initiative did not come from the black workers' legal or illegal labour organizations. The legal trade unions neither could nor would encourage the strikes. One trade union actually worked against the strikes. And yet, in those regions with the highest percentage of trade union organization, almost the total work force went on strike. The strikes during the third week of August indicate that the workers acknowledge the ANC as a leading force in the struggle for liberation. At the same time, it shows the effectiveness of the ANC's illegal networks in the townships. The fact that the ANC and the illegal trade union congress, SACTU, work very closely together is very important for SACTU's future work (see section 3.7 on SACTU's work).

The final essential difference is that while the Durban strikes were centered in the industrial areas where strike committees were formed, workers encouraged to go on strike etc., the Soweto strikes were focused on the black residential areas - the townships. In South Africa this form of action is called a 'stay-at-home strike'. It has often been used earlier, especially in the political struggle of 1950's. A stay-at-home strike means that the workers are far away from the areas where they actually have power and are feared, namely in the industrial areas and the white urban areas. Stay-at-home strikes are not necessarily the result of an organized trade union movement, nor do they necessarily promote such an organization. This is, however, usually the case if the starting point, rallying-ground and leadership are located in the industrial areas. An effective stay-at-home strike can be the result of a good organization in the streets or districts of the town. But, there are two problems involved here. Firstly, the townships are purposely built in a manner which should enable the police to repress any threat. As a rule, the townships can easily be sealed off and controlled by heavily armed police and the army. Secondly, stay-at-home strikes can easily lead to that the strikers and their supporters placing the greatest importance on political demands for self-government and improvements in the segregated areas, instead of e.g. demanding trade union rights and the abolishment of the Bantustan-system. The key to the problem is the danger that the black workers will be stripped of their role as industrial workers in the white areas.

All in all, the Soweto strikes, nevertheless, reflected the fighting spirit and the political solidarity of the black workers, even though the initiative did not come from the working class itself, and in spite of the fact that they were not able to link together political and economic demands. The illegal strikes were carried out even though they meant a loss of necessary income for the individual workers. Added to this is the risk of victimization and, ultimately, deportation to Bantustans or prison.

Finally, the Soweto uprising and strikes indicated the beginning of more vigorous and intensified industrial conflicts in the years ahead. Thousands of young people followed a very militant line and throughout the struggle they developed a high degree of political awareness and organizing ability. The Financial Mail wrote:

> "Today's Black youth are clearly far more militant than the youth of yesterday. What may happen when they themselves enter the labour force and start taking jobs in factories, mines and offices is a chastening thought."[15]

2.4 THE STRIKE WAVE IN 1980

The beginning of the 1980's witnessed an increase in the number of strikes in South Africa. In 1980 there were in total, according to official sources, 207 illegal strikes with a loss of 175,000 working-days. The second highest number of strikes since 1945.[16]

I will here examine and analyse five of the strikes which can be characterized as mass-action.[17]

1. The slaughterhouse-worker's strike -the 'meat-strike' - from the 8th of May to the 8th of August in 1980, in which approximately 800 workers from 15 factories took part.

2. The textile-workers' strike in Durban from the 22nd of May to the 1st of June 1980, which involved 5-7000 workers from 5 textile factories.

3. The 'remember the Soweto/76 strike' in Cape Town from the 16th to the 17th of June 1980 with some 50-80 % of worker support from the Cape Town area.

4. The automobile strike in Eastern Cape from the 14th/15th of June to the 7th of July, where nearly 10,000 workers from 10 automobile factories participated.

5. The <u>municipal-workers' strike</u> in Johannesburg from the 4th to the 31st of July 1980, which involved approximately 10,000 workers from nearly all departments of the municipal service (water, garbage collectors etc.).

I will begin with the <u>'remember Soweto strike'</u>, because there are some essential features which distinguish it from the other strikes. It has, however, many traits in common with the Soweto strikes of 1976. The preliminary stage of the strike took place at large public meetings, and the immediate support of both the coloured and the African workers is attributable to the fact that a large part of the population was mobilized already due to the meat-strike, a bus-boycott and a school-boycott, which earlier had led to the murder of two school children in the coloured section of the city by the police. It is not clear whether the initiative stemmed from any particular organization. However, it can be ascertained that the strike had broad support from the legal trade unions and residential groups in Cape Town.[18] The strike was planned as a peaceful manifestation: with only a moral condemnation of strike-breakers. However, on the 17th of June some school children threw stones at a bus filled with strike-breakers, and this resulted in brutal reaction from the heavily armed police. The peaceful demonstration was spontaneously transformed into one of the largest civil riots since the Soweto revolt in 1976.

On the 19th of June more than 40 people were killed and more than 200 wounded by police bullets.

The strike itself was a general political protest against the conditions the blacks are forced to live under in the apartheid system. To my knowledge no specific demands were made.

It was a common feature of the <u>other four strikes</u> that they were mainly concentrated within <u>one branch</u>, and all were <u>regionally rooted</u>. They distinguish themselves from the Durban and Soweto strikes in that there was more organizational work behind the initiative, execution and follow up of the strikes.

The background of the <u>meat-strike</u> was that the employers at two factories refused to recognize independent, and non-racial democratic committees. This triggered off sympathy strikes at the other abbatoirs. The strike was

led by a joint committee selected among the workers.
(Western Province) General Workers Union, GWU, helped the
committee and coordinated the support-work for the strike.
75-100 % of the workers at each slaughterhouse in Cape
Town were members of GWU[19] and all participated in the
strike. The strike was characterized by the close collaboration between the strikers and residential groups in the
African and the coloured townships.

The textile-workers' strike started when the workers at
one of the factories stopped work because of a fruitless
wage negotiation. On the same day the strike spread to
three other textile factories. During the 11 day strike
the workers' trade union, the National Union of Textile
Workers (NUTW), was able to hold two meetings with 5-6 000
strikers.

The municipal-workers' strike began after 500 power-station
workers were fired because they refused to work for current
wages. During the course of the strike the Black Municipality Workers Union, BMWU, played a major role in charting
the course of the strike, and acted as the representative
body for the strikers.

The automobile-workers' strike was similar to the three
other strikes in that it was not a planned mass strike
from the outset, but it became so, when the strike spread
out from one particular industry. The automobile workers
are relatively well organized, and the then trade union
for the coloureds, the National Union of Motor Assembly
and Rubber Workers of South Africa (NUMARWOSA) and the
trade union for the Africans, the United Auto Workers
(UAW) were able to negotiate on the workers' behalf. The
conflicts between different fractions of the members and
the two unions has later led to the formation of a new
automobile trade union in the area, and UAW & NUMARWOSA
have in 1980 merged together with a third automobile trade
union under NUMARWOSA's name.

As to the demands made during the strikes an increase in
salary played a central role in the strikes of the textile-
and automobile-workers. The textile-workers demanded and
won a 25 % increase in salary which was apportioned over 6
months. However, many of the most active workers were not
re-instated after the strike. The automobile-workers
demanded an increase in minimum-salary from Rand(R) 1.15

to R 2.- per hour, but they settled for R 1.45 per hour.
This was also an increase of approximately 25 % in salary.
In addition, the workers were promised an increase in
minimum-salary of up to R 2.- per hour at a later date. As
with the Durban strikes in 1973, the automobile-workers'
demand of an immediate increase to R 2.- must also be seen
as a political protest against a system which denies the
black workers a satisfactory standard of living.

As mentioned earlier, the municipal-workers' strike stemmed
from a wage dispute, but the strike also became a protest
against the municipal councils' refusal to recognize the
BMWU. Even though 2/3 (10,000 workers) of the working
force in the municipality went on strike the municipal
council would only recognize and negotiate with the Union
of Johannesburg Municipal Workers (UJMW). During the strike
when the government gave the UJMW a provisional registration it only had 40 paying members, in spite of the fact
that the municipal government had given the union leaders
free rein to organize the workers.[20] The municipal government broke the strike by deporting thousands of the
workers, who were mainly contract-workers, to different
bantustans. In addition, the president of the BMWU, Joe
Mavi, and other union leaders were accused of sabotage and
put in prison. Neither the demands for higher wages or the
recognition of BMWU were fulfilled.

Nor were the meat-workers able to make their employers
accept independent, non-racial and democratically chosen
labour committees in the factories. The standing of the
AWU in the community, however, increased significantly.

As to the question of whether the strikes were trials of
strength or demonstration-strikes, all four strikes must
be categorized as a test of strength, though with varying
length of time, according to the resources, intensity and
perception of the parties involved.
The employers' reply to the mass strikes varies. The meat-
bosses, the city-council in Johannesburg and the tex-
tile-employers categorically refuse to negotiate with trade
unions that reject or criticize the government's new system
of controlling the trade unions. By contrast employers
such as Ford seek to use the trade unions as a stabilizing
factor in the case of unrest or disturbances in the factory. For example, Ford is the first employer in South

Africa to introduce a system of full-time shop-stewards
who are paid by the company.

A significant factor in the 1980 strikes was active state
intervention. The authorities prohibited all gatherings,
meetings were broken up by tear gas and buckshots, the
striking workers were deported to the bantustans, union
leaders were arrested and charges were raised against the
strikers (to a greater extent than in the 1970's) for
merely striking.[21]

An important reason behind the tough line from the government was that the new labour legislation from 1979 would
be discredited if wage-demands and trade union recognitions
were carried through outside the official system.[22]

The strike wave in 1980 and the Durban strike had a basic
common feature which has not been discussed yet: the economic background. They both took place in a period where
the economy was experiencing a high rate of growth, but
where the real wages of the black workers were either
stagnating or directly falling as a consequence of the
high rate of inflation. In 1980 the rate of inflation was
about 20 %.[23] According to a survey the real wages of the
textile-workers fell by 15 % from 1977 to 1980.[24] The pur-
chasing power of the municipal workers was estimated to be
13 % lower in 1980 than it was in 1977.[25]

From 1973 to 1980 the reactions to these conditions have
changed, however. This gives the 1980 strikes a quali-
tatively different content than the Durban strikes.

While the Durban strikes were concentrated on economic
questions the 1980 strikes took place within a framework
of an expanding trade union organization, and they therefore, to a large extent, also expressed the problems of
this process; e.g. contradictions between the trade unions
on one side and the employers and the state on the other,
between different trade unions, and sometimes between trade
union members and their leaders. The political demand for
a recognition of non-racial, democratic, independent trade
unions and committees is also much clearer expressed than
during the Durban strikes.

Notes

1 See e.g. R. Hyman: Strikes, Glasgow 1977, pp. 19ff.

2 See Lenin: Strike Statistics in Russia, 1910, and R. Luxemburg; The Mass Strike, Young Socialist Publications, 1970.

3 See J.P. Sartre; Mass, Spontaneity, Party, London 1970 and J. P. Sartre, La Critique de la Raison Dialectique, Paris 1960. This point was put forth by Webster/Kuzwayo: Research Note on Consciousness and the Problem of Organization, p. 230 in Schlemmer/Webster: Change, Reform & Economic Growth in South Africa, Johannesburg 1978.

4 The Durban Strikes, Ravan Press, 1976 is indisputably the major work in the analysis of the Durban strikes, and has contributed much to the discussion of the Durban strikes in this report. In addition, see also the discussion on the Durban strikes in C. du Toit: Capital & Labour in South Africa - Class Struggles in the 1970's, Holland, 1981.

5 There was a 40 % increase in the standard of living from 1971-73 (Poverty Datum Line, PDL) for the average black family, according to P.N. Pillay: A Poverty Datum Line Study among Africans In Durban, University of Natal, 1973, P. 22; quoted from D. Hemson: "Trade Unionism and the Struggle for Liberation in South Africa", Capital & Class, 6, 1978, p. 18f.

6 The principal content of the investigation can be summarized as follows:
   1. Awareness of the fact that solidarity is necessary in order to change conditions .... 70 %
   2. Awareness of the potential of combined strength . 50 %
   3. Clear class-based political awareness .... 27 %
   4. A definite understanding of the necessity for political and/or trade union action .... 10 %
   5. A feeling of powerlessness as opposed to the state and employers .... 40 %
   Sources: L. Schlemmer: The African Industrial Worker View his Situation, in D. Horner: Labour Organization and the African Worker, Johannesburg 1974. See also The Durban Strikes, op. cit., p. 57.

7 The Durban Strikes, op. cit. p. vi.

8 In order to make an appraisal of this it is necessary to point out that the workers' economic demands are not necessarily economistic. It is only an economistic struggle if it is reduced to a question of merely sharing the gains from increased productivity to the exclusion of political demands. The existence of political demands is, on the other hand, not in itself a sufficient criterium to make it revolutionary. It will depend on whether or not such political demands may be accommodated within the existing order through reforms. Only to the extent political demands are so radical that their fulfillment requires a fundamental change of the prevailing system, can a struggle carrying demands of that nature be termed revolutionary. A revolutionary struggle cannot, however, be limited to political demands alone. It is of utmost importance to fight simultaneously for reforms within the system in order to achieve immediate improvements in workers' wages and working conditions etc.

9   See J. Kane-Berman: South Africa - The Method in the Madness, London 1979; Brooke/Brickhill: Whirlwind before the Storm, IDAF, London 1980, or D. Herbstein: White Man, We Want to Talk to You, Essex, 1978.

10 Mafeje: 'Soweto and its Aftermath', Review of African Political Economy, 11, 1979, p. 19.

11 Ibid. p. 19.

12 A Survey of Race Relations in South Africa. 1976, Johannesburg, 1977.

13 In Callinicos/Rogers; Southern Africa after Soweto, London 1977, p. 165, it is reported that a journalist from Rand Daily Mail overheard a conversation in which a police officer said to some Zulu migrant workers who had burned down buildings, "We didn't order you to destroy property. You were asked to fight people only".

14 A Survey of Race Relations in South Africa, op.cit., p. 80.

15 Financial Mail, Aug. 6, 1976.

16 Financial Mail, May 8, 1981.

17 Whether a strike is a mass strike or not has primarily not anything to do with the number of workers that are involved, but is rather determined by how the strike spreads and the percentage of factories involved in a given industrial branch or geographical region.

    In two of the strikes discussed, the workers had the same employers; namely the Frame concern and the municipal council in Johannesburg.

18 Financial Mail, June 6, 1980.

19 South African Labour Bulletin, Jan. 6, 1980, p. 77.

20 Work in Progress, Sept. 14, 1980, p. 45; South African Labour Bulletin 6 & 7, 1981, p. 8, in an article by J. Keenan: 'Migrants Awake' - the 1980 Johannesburg Municipal Strike.

21 For example, 298 of the textile workers were charged for participation in the strike, cf. Work in Progress, Sept. 14, 1980, p. 53.

22 National Manpower Commission stated in its Annual Report of 1980 that: "Statistics are not available (but) it is known that nearly all trade unions involved (in strikes) were unregistered", Source: Financial Mail July 10, 1981.

23 Work in Progress, April 17, 1981, p. 27.

24 FOSATU Workers News, no. 5, June 1980.

25 Work in Progress, Sept. 14, 1980, p. 46.

3. LABOUR ORGANIZATION

3.1 INTRODUCTION

On the basis of a structuralist approach to the understanding of organizations, it can be said that in social formations one will find looser or more permanent associations of individuals, organizations that can be analysed within an organization's sphere, which again is part of the sphere of the total class struggle. The organizations in society can develop into a relatively independent structure with a decisive influence on the development of the total class struggle.

In a concrete analysis of organizations, it is essential to investigate the degree of consciousness of common class interests and the organization's 'isolation-neutralizing practice', i.e. whether the organization acts as a vehicle towards increasing the members' awareness that they have a common interest. An analysis must also attempt to locate the position of the organization in relation to the fundamental structures of the society, and to explain against which part of the society's structure the organization directs its activities. In addition, the organization's dependence and influence on non-organized class practice should be analysed. Following this, it is important to investigate the organization's internal resources, structure and its relation to its members.

This provides the general framework for a closer analysis of the specific type of organization that the research focusses on. Here the task is to determine what it is in the capitalist society's structures that give rise to trade unions and in what context they operate.

The primary purpose of trade unions is to attend to the interests of its members in the reproduction of their manpower. The monopolization of the supply and sale of labour, together with the threat of withdrawing the same (strikes) are essential to the success of this work. Trade unions and the constant wage-struggle are the preconditions for improving the living standard of the working class in the capitalist system. However, when workers unite in a class-organization as an answer to or defense against exploitation, they are also preparing the groundwork for an offensive use of these organizations, not only for wage improvements, but also for the implementation of radical changes in the existing organization of production.

It is of vital importance, therefore, to analyse the trade unions' perception of the relation between economic and political work, and their practices in both spheres.

3.2 THE OVERALL PICTURE

The black workers' trade union struggle in South Africa have historically come in waves. The peaks have been the 1920's, 1940's and around 1960. From the beginning of the 1970's the black trade unions have again increased their following constantly (from 1970 to 1981 the number of black union members has increased from approximately 15,000 to well over 150,000). In between, i.e. in the 1930's, around 1950 and in the 1960's the state and employers have succeeded in suppressing the black workers' potential to organize themselves. The oscillations can best be defined as offensive and defensive periods of the trade union movement. In this research report I will concentrate on the latest offensive from 1970 and onwards, and within this I will focus on the situation at the beginning of the 1980's. For a fuller historical account I refer the reader to other works.[1]

The principal legal unions which consist mainly of black workers within the manufacturing industry and service sector are:[2]
- the TUCSA-affiliated black trade unions,
- The Council of Unions of South Africa (CUSA),
- The Federation of South African Trade Unions (FOSATU),
- The independent trade unions.

Added to this is the underground trade union organization South African Congress of Trade Unions (SACTU).

3.3 THE TUCSA-AFFILIATED TRADE UNIONS

The Trade Union Council of South Africa was established in 1954 and consisted of registered trade unions. The members were white, coloured, and Indians. Trade unions with predominantly black members were excluded. The TUCSA-unions directly or indirectly supported the government's attempt to split the trade union movement on a racial basis. Since then, TUCSA has permitted and forbidden admission of black workers three times. In 1973 TUCSA requested its members to form parallel trade unions for blacks within their specific field. Approximately a year later, 1974, TUCSA opened its doors and allowed black trade unions to become members. In 1979/80, after the black trade unions were allowed to be registered, TUCSA has intensified its efforts to form parallel labour unions. Several TUCSA affiliated unions have also attained a multi-racial status so that the blacks may become members, but only in a particular division of the union.

The reason behind TUCSA's efforts in the 1970's to admit blacks to the organization is that TUCSA has become less and less representative of the total working force, due to the rapid growth in the number of blacks on the labour market. This means that TUCSA's bargaining position with the employers will increasingly become weakened if they do not, one way or another, try to include the blacks in the organization. TUCSA is also interested in organizing the blacks from a political and ideological perspective because it fears the political potential of the growing black trade union movement. The control is quite obvious in the former all-white trade unions since the organizations' apparatus remains unchanged. The situation is, however, basically the same in the parallel trade unions. In spite of their formal independent status. In the guidelines which TUCSA's Secretary General, Grobbelaars, has given for the administration of the parallel-labour unions he states that: 'Administration should continue to be subject to overall supervision by the registered union'.[3]

As a rule, the parallel trade unions do not have their own premises or independent administration, and very often they have the same Secretary General as the 'mother-labour union'.

That TUCSA's parallel-labour unions are utilized to counter-act the activities of the independent black trade unions was for example exposed in 1973 when TUCSA started a parallel-labour union (African Transport Workers Union) a week after the independent Transport & Allied Workers Union was formed. This was done precisely in the same area. In

1979 in a memorandum FOSATU, pointed out how the parallel-labour unions are increasingly being used to out-manoeuvre the independent black trade unions.[4] In 1980 the security police in East London prepared a report which, as one of the countermoves to the increasing radicalization of the black trade unions, suggested that TUCSA's parallel-unions be established in the region:

> "To obtain a more even balance, one would have to activate and motivate TUCSA to show more interest and to be more active insofar as recruitment and organiz-ation of workers is concerned."[5]

Regarding the TUCSA-affiliated trade unions' policy, I will try to illustrate it by reference to the National Union of Clothing Workers (NUCW). It is by far the largest parallel-union with 16,000 members, and has as an exception its own black Secretary General, Lucy Mvubelo. In 1956 NUCW decided to withdraw from the then umbrella-organization South African Congress of Trade Unions (SACTU), which consisted mainly, but not exclusively, of black trade unions.

The reason was that SACTU wanted to establish closer ties with the blacks' political mass organization, the African National Congress (ANC). In this connection Lucy Mvubelo said that: "Politics was a death-knell to us."[6] In 1959, NUCW helped to start the Federation of Free African Trade Unions of South Africa (FOFATUSA) to counteract the in-fluence of SACTU. FOFATUSA "... was opposed to the SACTU position that trade unionism and politics was insepar-able".[7] The trade unions that affiliated to FOFATUSA had to agree to limit themselves to work with only 'worker grievances'. In 1975, Lucy Mvubelo along with TUCSA, assured the government that they would support the govern-ment "in stopping Communist infiltration into the labour force".[8] In an attempt to attain official recognition, Lucy Mvubelo, maintained in 1974 that NUCW had never en-couraged the black workers to strike, and 'if strikes occurred they usually lasted up to the time when one of the union's officials arrived on the scene."[9]

This economistic interpretation of the labour struggle is reflected in the reaction of TUCSA-affiliated trade unions to the Wiehahn Commission's proposal in 1979 for recog-nized, but government-controlled, trade unions. Lucy Mvubelo stated that the original suggestions in the Com-mission's Report were:

'recommendations that caused great rejoicing among black trade unionists. We felt as though we had hit the jack-pot'. 'I know that giving the black workers their first full opportunity for bargaining is funda-mental - not cosmetic'. 10

On the international scene NUCW has tried to prevent all support to SACTU and is actively trying to prevent an economic boycott of South Africa.

In summary, TUCSA's primary purpose in encouraging the blacks to join the organization is to preserve the white workers' privileged position, and to control and dominate the ever growing black trade union movement. The parallel-unions are under organizational control and are subjected to the economistic line that characterizes the TUCSA-unions.

Whether this is representative of all the approximately 25,000 African workers in the TUCSA-affiliated trade unions is still an open question. But the mass-strikes that took place in 1976 indicate that this is not the case. In the areas where NUCW is strongest many black workers partici-pated actively in the strikes. The reason for this, accord-ing to D. Hemson, is the work of the nearly 300 women shop-stewards who are active in the labour struggle at the 'grass root' level, and to some extent act independently of the leadership of the union. Whether this will have any significant consequences for the future role of the TUCSA-affiliated unions is difficult to say at the present time.[11]

3.4 THE COUNCIL OF UNIONS OF SOUTH AFRICA (CUSA)

CUSA was established in 1980. It has eight affiliated trade unions comprising in all nearly 45,000 members.[12] The CUSA-unions organize only black workers. Generally, the trade unions are either parallel-unions that have with-drawn from the 'mother-union', or independent unions that were established with the support of Urban Training Project (UTP). UTP is an advisory organ for black trade unions. It was established in 1970 by white intellectuals who were dissatisfied with TUCSA's vacillating politics towards black trade unions. From 1973 until 1980 the unions that are now attached to CUSA and other trade unions in the Witwatersrand region had established some loose cooperation in 'the Consultative Committee of Black Trade Unions' (CC). This organization was seriously undermined when five of

the affiliated-unions took part in the creation of the
Federation of South African Trade Unions (FOSATU). In many
of CC's labour unions there was a disagreement between the
permanently employed secretary general, who was against
FOSATU, and the majority of the members and elected leaders
who were in favour of joining FOSATU. The establishment of
CUSA in September 1980 - after one year's preparation -
must clearly be seen as an attempt to counteract the
influence of FOSATU.

There are three reasons why CUSA preferred to stand apart
from FOSATU. Firstly, the CUSA-unions wished to prevent
outside bodies such as the Institute for Industrial Education, Industrial Aid Society (and UTP) from negotiating
the establishment of FOSATU. Secondly, the CUSA-unions
wanted the Trade Union Advisory and Coordinating Committee
(TUACC), which was the umbrella for black trade unions in
Durban and the force behind the establishment of FOSATU,
to make a binding agreement not to establish any of its
unions in the Johannesburg region where there was a possi-
bility that they would compete with the already existing
trade unions. Thirdly, CUSA, not very precisely, stated
that the federation of trade unions should be strong, and
that there should be no obstacles which would prevent the
development of a 'black leadership'. These conditions,
according to the CUSA-unions, were not fulfilled by the
establishment of FOSATU.

FOSATU for its part has criticized CUSA-unions for being too
leader-controlled and putting too much emphasis on communication between the leadership of the trade unions and the
employers, instead of organizing the labour force at the
'grass-root' level in the enterprises. Another point of
criticism is that CUSA-labour unions only admit membership
of blacks, and consequently widen the distance between the
races in the labour movement. Whether the CUSA-unions
follow an economistic or a more revolutionary line in
their work can be illustrated by the attitude of the UTP
to this question. The CUSA-unions are closely connected to
the UTP because many of them as mentioned were formed by
the UTP and UTP still renders them for instance, vocational
training. UTP makes a sharp distinction between the trade
union and the political struggle and states that their
work is apolitical.

The black trade unions, according to UTP, must be supported, so that they can "... establish mutually satisfactory relationships with employers" (My emphasis, jh). It was expressed elsewhere that "UTP and the black workers are first and foremost concerned with the building up of a healthy relationship with the employers". (My emphasis, jh).

This 'class cooperation' policy was set forth again by UTP in connection with the banning of L.D. Dekker in 1976:

> "Why should a faithful citizen like Loet (D. Dekker) who has on so many occasions opposed boycotts against South Africa be separated from his life long ambition? ... Why should the founder member of UTP, an organization geared for better employer-employee relationships in South Africa be accused of underground activities while the contrary is true?"

It should be underlined that the approach that UTP is trying to advance is contrary to, and restrains a more radical reaction among the black workers:

> "... authorities must realize (by the banning of UTP members, jh) that they are instrumental in bringing about economic and political chaos. They should know that there are elements waiting for such opportunities where black workers can be used to further their aims and objectives."

UTP receives significant support from abroad, among which are Christian trade unions in Holland, Switzerland, and West Germany. UTP stressed heavily that this support should be seen in the light of the organization's attempt to create "mutually satisfactory relationship with employers".

The general impression is that UTP does not utilize the possibilities that - in spite of all difficulties - do exist for raising the perspective beyond the 'bread and butter' level.

Moreover, UTP places far too much emphasis on the economic character of the trade union struggle than would have been the case if it was only a tactic it was forced to follow because of the restrictive conditions for trade union work.

CUSA's constitution, however, does to some extent allow the trade unions to express themselves politically. For example about ILO's working norms and the workers' social conditions. According to its own perception, CUSA also has a vital role to play in the development of 'black leaders'. In CUSA's view, only these can guarantee the creation of a 'non-racial, nonexploitative, democratic society'.[14]

P. Camay, secretary general of CUSA, expresses CUSA's attitude towards political questions as follows:

> ""CUSA is not seeking direct confrontation with the
> state on political issues. We believe appropriate
> organizations exist in the community with a cour-
> ageous and able leadership which can look after the
> political aspirations of the Black worker". 15

CUSA will, at the same time, according to Camay, actively
fight against any political interference in the affairs of
the trade unions.

CUSA does not appear to have a perspective that transcends
capitalist relations of production. The contents of a
'Policy Document' in 1981 indicate this:

> "CUSA believes in a free and just society and accepts
> the truism that <u>labour cannot exist without manage-
> ment.</u> 16 (My emphasis, jh.)

CUSA has not taken a position on the question of registration. All of CUSA's affiliated unions, however, have applied for registration, but only four were approved by the
authorities (in mid 1981). The other unions have yet to
receive a reply. CUSA's affiliated unions have not made
any conditions for being registered. FOSATU has asserted
that it was quite impossible to get CUSA to co-operate in
forming a common front among the independent black labour
unions against the labour market legislation of 1979.

To summarize, the CUSA-unions distinguish themselves by
being independent of TUCSA, but in trade union policy they
follow an economistic line and their organized base is not
as developed as that of other independent labour unions.
The establishment of independent organizations in a repressive system such as South Africa, sometimes represents a
step forward - regardless of the specific line the trade
unions follow.

This line, however, becomes a central problem when trade
unions are faced with suggestions for reform, as happened
in South Africa in 1979. Here CUSA's predominant economistic line led to the acceptance of working within a framework which will make it very difficult for the trade
unions to meet the demands of their members; both for
better wages and working conditions and more long-term
changes in the social structure of society.

3.5   FEDERATION OF SOUTH AFRICAN TRADE UNIONS (FOSATU)

FOSATU is a federation of 12 labour unions with a total of
more than 50,000 members.[17] It was formed in the spring of
1979. The trade unions come from three main groups; firstly
the TUACC group (Trade Union Advisory and Coordinating
Committee) which was a co-ordinating organ for the trade
unions that arose out of the Durban strikes in 1973, secondly,
the Consultative Committee of Trade Unions in Johannesburg, which was split on the question of becoming an aff-
iliate of FOSATU, and thirdly , a group consisting of registered trade unions for coloured from the Cape Province.

There are several interesting aspects to FOSATU. First, as
opposed to CUSA, FOSATU is open to all races. Secondly, it
was the first time since the boom in the establishment of
legal trade unions in the beginning of the 1970's that an
organization was able to form a country-wide amalgamation
of legal trade unions. Until 1979 the trade unions were
split into regional groups. TUACC had its headquarters in
Natal, Consultative Committee in Transvaal, whereas there
were no such federations in the Cape Province. In relation
to the unions that remained in the Consultative Committee,
FOSATU clearly became the most dominant in Transvaal and
Natal. In Cape, FOSATU was much weaker, but it did have a
foot-hold in the automobile industry in Port Elizabeth and
Cape Town.

The third aspect is FOSATU's basic approach. Firstly,
FOSATU's formal structure allows for a relatively high
degree of control of the organization by its members. In
order to ensure factory-level support all the organs consist of a majority of workers, and the emphasis of its
activities is at the regional level, to be as close to the
members as possible. Furthermore FOSATU's basic structure
is designed in a manner that would enable it to develop a
strong organization at each individual firm or sector. It
was stated at FOSATU's first congressional meeting,

> "That FOSATU will assist its affiliates in the build-
> ing and consolidation of membership and stable shop
> floor committee structures in the factory leading to
> the winning of recognition and negotiating rights from
> management.
>
> - that such recognition and negotiating rights should
>   be achieved at both industrial and plant level.

> - that the essential basis for such rights is the re-
> cognition at plant level." 18

The "grass-root" policy was also characteristic of the
former TUACC labour unions whereas the FOSATU unions, which
originated from the Consultative Committee, had been criticized for being led too much from the 'top'. It is also
especially one of these unions, the UAW, that has had
problems in developing a "grass-root" policy. Repeated confrontations between the leadership and the majority of the
members led, in the beginning of 1981, to the formation of
a new independent union for the automobile workers in Port
Elizabeth.

Some of the independent trade unions have argued that to
work as a team in FOSATU drained the member-unions of
their resources to the extent that they neglected the
factory floor. In addition, they held that the member
unions could not properly plan and control the activities
in FOSATU which therefore were increasingly being led by
those who are permanently employed.

The fourth interesting aspect is that FOSATU is aware that
the trade union struggle to a certain extent involves
political issues. FOSATU's constitution states that it is
its duty:

> "- To comment on, advance or oppose any policy of any
> authority or institution affecting worker interest
> generally and the interest of the labour movement in
> particular." (Emphasis is mine, jh). 19

At FOSATU's congressional meeting, it was, however, stated
that:

> "FOSATU does not subscribe to, support or align itself
> with any party political organization ..." (My em-
> phasis, jh). 20

The crux of the matter in evaluating FOSATU's political
engagement is how to interpret the "worker interest generally and the interest of the labour movement in particular."
Is this solely a question of the conditions on the labour
market or does it also include the total living conditions
of the workers', for example as inhabitants in the slum
areas or pass-bearers? A. Erwin, Secretary General of
FOSATU, elaborated on this in 1979/80 in the following
manner:

"The key political issue is the problems affecting
workers. We'll speak out on those. But we are rather
conscious in some senses for two reasons. One is
definitely - one has to be realistic - it is a very
powerful and nervous state that doesn't like trade
unions talking about politics, but there is a second
reason which also is important - we don't want just
to make political statements that have no real impact.
Our prime task is to organize workers so they themselves can talk actively for what they want, which
hasn't been the case in the past." 21

Another common FOSATU argument against involving itself
with issues outside the labour market proper, is that it
would compromise the 'pure' working class base on which it
rests, because FOSATU would have to make alliances with
other types of organizations, for example, committees for
better housing.

FOSATU's attitude towards this question seems to be some-
what contradictory. On the one side FOSATU believes that
the conditions of the workers are decisive for the future
and that the organization should express the demands of
the workers. On the other side FOSATU is reluctant because
it fears the reaction of the state. Also, FOSATU believes
that it will be exploited in a co-operative relation with
other organizations. What if the workers' demands in fact
fall outside labour market issues? Would FOSATU attempt to
block or discourage this? It is also not difficult to
imagine that FOSATU could very well work together with
other organizations, and yet still maintain its own ident-
ity, if FOSATU beforehand made it clear to all what its
conditions or premises were for such cooperation.

An example of how FOSATU was more concerned about its
survival than taking a clear position is the question of
union registration under the labour market legislation of
1979. Even though FOSATU, in prinicple, argued that union
registration should only contain information concerning the
number of members, financial position and union rules, all
the non-registered FOSATU unions nevertheless sent in their
registration application in the spring of 1980. FOSATU
did, however, put up some demands for accepting the registration. The most important of these was that the unions
attained a multi-racial status. Previously, FOSATU, as it
was mentioned earlier, had attempted in vain to obtain a
common line with that of CUSA regarding the question of
registration. FOSATU was quick to agree with the rest of

the progressive labour unions in criticizing the new laws, but not on a common reply. Moreover, FOSATU was apparently not at all interested in forming a common front against registration along with other unions at that time. According to FOSATU this would not "create a significant joint stand in the eyes of management, government, and the international trade unions."[22] In all probability FOSATU was afraid that the government would encroach upon the activities of the non-registered unions, and was afraid of competition from registered CUSA- and TUCSA-affiliated unions. Furthermore, FOSATU trade unions were, because of economic difficulties, very much interested in attaining stop-order facilities, which the employers threatened to deny them as long as they did not register.

FOSATU's dilemma becomes clear here, because the advantages that can be gained by registering must be compared with the purpose of the new legislation, which is to control the independent unions, and this control will make it very difficult to attend to the interests of the members.
At the same time, FOSATU compromises itself in the eyes of the black workers by becoming a part of an institution created by the apartheid government. FOSATU probably misinterpreted the situation in 1979 and 1980. The independent non-registered trade unions have since then been subject to selective intervention by the state, but they have not been forbidden, and their clear refusal to register and their political position has attracted more and more members so that they have nearly twice as many members as CUSA in 1981.

In the spring of 1981 five FOSATU trade unions attained registered union status, but all with limitations in what races they were allowed to organize. FOSATU has appealed this decision to the courts.

FOSATU has not (until 1981) suffered from imprisonment or banning of its leaders. Activists in member unions have, however, experienced detentions. The state also tried to strangle the organization economically in the summer of 1980 by depriving FOSATU of the right to receive economic aid from foreign countries. Nevertheless, FOSATU survived, but had to make a 40 % reduction in their activities (production of teaching materials, courses, legal aid, etc.)

To sum up, the establishment of FOSATU in 1979 signified an obvious strengthening of the position of the dominated classes. There is, nevertheless, a danger that FOSATU's understanding of the relation between trade union and political work and whether the trade unions can remain exempt from government control, will not match the changing political environment.

From 1981 it appears that different FOSATU unions seem to advocate different political lines of action. It is uncertain which course will be dominant in future, but FOSATU's participation in a protest meeting on August 8th, 1981 with the independent trade unions and CUSA, where a new labour market legislation was strongly criticized, and FOSATU's participation, with the independent labour unions, in a protest against bantustan policy in September 1981, suggests that FOSATU is gradually forced to broaden its interpretation of "worker and labour interest".[23]

3.6 THE INDEPENDENT TRADE UNIONS

The most important trade unions within this category are:[24]
- General Workers' Union, GWU, (approx. 12,000 members)
- Food & Canning Workers' Union/African Food & Canning Workers' Unions, F&C, (nearly 25,000 members)
- South African Allied Workers' Union, SAAWU, (approx. 20,000 members),
- Motor Assembly & Component Workers' Union of South Africa, MACWUSA, (approx. 6,000 members),
- General Workers' Union of South Africa, GAWUSA, (approx. 2,000 members),
- Black Municipality Workers' Union, BMWU, (approx. 11,000 members),
- General and Allied Workers' Union, GAWU, (approx. 5,000 members).

These unions have a total of over 80,000 members. Most of these unions are relatively new. Only GWU and F&C existed prior to 1979. F&C was established in the 1940's, but it was only after 1976 that the organization was able to overcome the effect of the recession in the 1960's. GWU grew out of a workers' advisory office which began in 1973 in Cape Town.[25] The other trade unions were established between 1979 and 1981.

Even though the relations between these unions have not been formalized there are nevertheless many similarities between them, and they will therefore be dealt with as one. In addition, the unions very often have informal relations in those cities where several of them are represented; for example, in East London.

All of the unions are multi-racial, and voice very clearly a class-based understanding of the social order. The Vice-President of SAAWU, Sisa Njikelana, expressed this in the following manner;

> ""We are not struggling against a particular race, creed, or religion. We are toiling against the exploiters and oppressors irrespective of colour." 26

The grass-root orientation among these unions was expressed by GWU as follows:

> ""It is necessary to recognize that the unusual strength of the unregistered unions ... rest precisely in the democratic functioning of the unions; it rests precisely on the fact that our unions are controlled by the workers." 27

While F&C and GWU strongly emphasize the significance of democratic structures and procedures in their daily functions, SAAWU and MACWUSA especially stress the importance of mass participation in the decision-making process of the unions. They call it 'mass participatory democracy', and it seems that, on and off, they have been able to hold discussion-meetings where thousands of the members have been present. One feature which is common to all the independent trade unions is their attempt to strengthen grass-root democracy and to develop members' ability to solve problems themselves by establishing independent, nonracial, and democratically elected committees at the factory floor.

As mentioned earlier, one of the independent unions, MACWUSA, was established because the then trade union, United Auto Workers (UAW) had little contact with the shop-floor organization and perceived the workers' independent and well formulated demands as a threat to, rather than a boost to the union.[28]

As to the question of integrating political questions in trade union work, the independent unions feel that it is necessary to raise both the local and the national political questions in their work. With regard to the local problems, G. Zini from MACWUSA stated that: "If there is a problem in the community, we will be involved."[29]

At the GWU conference in 1981, it was made very clear that they would also not hesitate to involve themselves in 'community affairs'.[30] The President of SAAWU, T. Gweta, stated in 1981 that SAAWU would work together with community organizations, and if necessary take the intitiative in forming such. He further added that these groups could be an indispensable support for workers on strike if consumer-boycotts had to be started or money collected for a strike-fund.[31] The Fatti & Moni strike in 1979, the meatworkers strike in 1980, and the Wilson- Rowntree conflict in 1981 are good illustrations of the teamwork between the striking workers and community organizations. In regard to the national political questions, GWU stated in 1981:

> "we would wish to preserve the right to affiliate to a political party or 'political organization' should the members so wish" 32

GWU further stressed the important role of the workers in the decision-making process:

> "We will work for the right of workers to participate fully in the democratic government of the country because workers are the people who produce the country's wealth." 33

Regarding the organized working class's political role, SAAWU states in its constitution that:

> "Only the working class, in alliance with other progressive minded sections of the community, can build a happy life for all South Africans ..." 34

SAAWU-leaders put it this way in an interview in 1981:

> "... the movement of the workers (...) are aimed at the total liberation of the working class and the toiling masses in this country." 35

A resolution at the SAAWU conference in 1981 demanded the release of Nelson Mandela from prison, and maintained that he is recognized as the national leader.[36] But until now, none of the unions have attempted to match such words with deeds.

The trade unions' attitude towards the government's attempt to regulate the labour market from 1979 until the present is due to their conception of the unions' internal democracy and their role in the political struggle. Their attitude is that the registration of unions will make it impossible for the workers to control their own destiny and will, furthermore, prevent them from taking a political position when and where they themselves decide. Because of

this they absolutely refused to be registered. GWU stated
that:

> "If we hand over to the state the right to control
> our unions then surely we are behaving in a manner
> which is not only unprincipled, but is ultimately
> self-defeating, for we shall be removing the very
> basis of our strength - the fullest participation of
> the workers in control of their unions." 37

SAAWU made it clear that it would not subject itself to
any form of legal regulations as long as the central
elements in the apartheid system are maintained:

> "If we agreed to become part of the system, we would
> be agreeing to abide by all the laws which hinder the
> blacks. We demand such laws be removed. Only then we
> will consider registration." 38

None of the unions have applied for registration. It was
these unions, particularly GWU, which were the main force
behind the meeting on August 8th, 1981 in Cape Town between
FOSATU and CUSA unions, where a joint statement was issued,
which strongly criticized the labour market legislation.

The independent trade unions have been involved in almost
all of the conflicts on the labour market in 1979-81. In
addition to the Futti & Moni, meat-workers' & Wilson-Rown-
tree conflicts. I will mention the previously discussed
municipal workers' strike and the Firestone conflict in
1981, which involved sympathy strikes at Ford and General
Motors.

The repression of the trade unions has often taken the
form of arrests of the leaders and the most active members.
As a rule they were released some time later without being
charged for anything specific, or if there were charges,
they were later withdrawn. There have been very few instan-
ces of a case being brought to court. During the first six
months of 1981 over 60 SAAWU's leaders and active members
were arrested and put in prison for shorter or longer
periods of time. The leaders of GWU and BMWU were also
arrested during the meat-workers' and the municipality
workers' strikes in 1980. No charges were raised against
the leaders of GWU, and they were acquitted after the
conflicts came to an end. But the state started a case
against the President of BMWU, Joe Mavi. He was acquitted,
but the legal process continued until the spring of 1981.
From the latter part of May 1981 until the time this is
written (October 1981) three of MACWUSA's leaders were

imprisoned for terrorism, but no precise charges were brought against them.

In addition to this, the state interferes by sending representatives to industries that are in conflict with the workers, and advise the employers not to negotiate with workers before they resume their work again. The Minister of Manpower Fannie Botha, urged the employers in 1980 to stand together against SAAWU and F & C until the government put into effect a more restrictive policy for non-registered trade unions.[39] In addition, it was revealed that the security police, as mentioned, have worked out a report to the employers which - among other things - requests them to exploit the very high unemployment rate in East London as weapon against the independent trade unions. In order to avoid this and also to preserve the membership of its sacked members, SAAWU started a trade union for the unemployed - the first of its kind in South Africa.

It is not certain what methods of repression the government will use against the independent trade unions in the future, but the proposed amendment to the labour legislation from the autumn of 1981 coupled with a statement from Erasmus,[40] the chief of the Security Police in Port Elizabeth, indicates that the security police will be used to a greater degree against the independent progressive trade unions. According to Erasmus, the state will no longer tolerate illegal strikes or the boycott of consumer-goods. The labour legislation will be discussed in detail in chapter four .

3.7 SOUTH AFRICAN CONGRESS OF TRADE UNIONS (SACTU)

SACTU was formed in 1955. The initiative came from 14 minor progressive trade unions who refused to take part in the establishment of TUCSA. Instead they chose to work together with the Council of Non-European Trade Unions (CNETU) - an umbrella organ for black trade unions.[44] In the years that followed 17 black unions joined SACTU, and 12 new ones were formed. In 1961, when SACTU membership reached its peak, the number of affiliated unions was 46 (of which 36 were black), and the total number of members was 53,323 (498 whites, 12,384 coloured, 1,650 Indians, and 38,791 blacks). At that time SACTU had 65 permanently employed organizers or secretaries.

There are some traits which distinguish SACTU's work from earlier attempts to organize labour. The most important feature was the consistent acknowledgement of the close relationship between the trade union and the political struggle. Of course, there have been trade unions before with the same perspective. The CNETU, for example, supported the 'Defiance Campaign' in the beginning of the 1950's. What distinguishes SACTU is how it makes this perspective an integrated part of its platform and practice. This is clearly spelled out in a resolution from the first national congress of SACTU in 1956:

> "SACTU is conscious of the fact that the organizing of the mass of the workers for higher wages, better conditions of life and labour is inextricably bound up with a determined struggle for political rights and liberation from all oppressive laws and practices. It follows that a mere struggle for the economic rights of the workers without participation in the general struggle for political emancipation would condemn the trade union movement to uselessness and to a betrayal of the interests of the workers." 42

The long-term goal of SACTU's work was expressed in the following manner by one of its leaders in 1955:

> "Now comrades, the biggest difficulty we are facing in South Africa is that one of capitalism in all its oppressive measures versus the ordinary people - the ordinary workers in the country. We find in this country ... the means of production, the factories, the lands, the industries, and everything possible is owned by a small group of people who are the capitalists in this country. They skin the people, they live off the fat of the workers and make them work, as a matter of fact in exploitation. They oppress in order to keep them as slaves, in the land of their births.
>
> Now, friends, this is a very important demand in the Freedom Charter. Now we would like to see a South Africa where the industries, the land, the big business and the mines, and everything that is owned by a small group of people in this country, must be owned by all the people in this country. That is what we demand, and that is what we fight for ...". 43

There can be no doubt that SACTU was quite aware that a central task of the trade unions was to combat the capitalist system which relies on exploitation. The racial suppression of the black workers is only seen as a form of capitalism in South Africa and not as the essence of the system:

> "That in fact apartheid serves the interests of capitalism. That it rests on the exploitation of the working class. That its basic function is to control

labour. That, in short, apartheid is today nothing less than a method by which capitalism exploits cheap labour under the special conditions, which exist in South Africa." 44

It was this understanding of class oppression and the integration of the economic and the political struggle that caused SACTU to join the 'Congress Alliance' in 1955. In the same year SACTU endorsed its programme - the Freedom Charter - which stipulated the basic demands of the organizations for a liberated South Africa. For instance, SACTU participated in the campaigns of the 1950's against the pass laws and the more and more rigid division of the country into black and white areas. SACTU was also involved in the organization of 'stay-at-home' strikes as a means of supporting these demands. This does not mean that the members' immediate material demands were ignored. On the contrary, SACTU started a campaign for a minimum wage of 2 Rand per day, supported affiliated trade unions through training courses, and was as mentioned responsible for the establishment of many trade unions. [45]

SACTU's policy was both the only logical answer to the obvious political obstacles which had been designed to prevent the organization of black workers throughout the century and represented a threat to the basic social structures upon which the system rested. The government had introduced the Native Labour (Settlement of Disputes) Act in 1953 as a desperate attempt to prevent the black workers from paralyzing the economy in order to back up their political demands. As SACTU nevertheless continued to take up political issues it was constantly harassed by the state. Right from the start SACTU's offices were frequently stormed and ransacked by the police. A large number of labour leaders were banned from their union duties. Out of the 156 people who were arrested under the 'Treason Trial' in 1956, 23 were SACTU mambers. After the 'stay-at-home' strikes in 1958, many of SACTU activists were arrested and sentenced to prison for encouraging the strikes. Following the banning of ANC and PAC in 1960 the state intensified the arrests and banning of SACTU activists, and in 1964 all of the leading members were affected by these measures.

It naturally follows that SACTU could not fulfil its role as a coordinating organization for the affiliated trade

unions, and consequently, SACTU gave up the legal struggle.
An illegal organisation was considered to be the only
realistic alternative for the future. SACTU has never been
officially forbidden. The reason for this is probably the
government's methods of repression in the form of arrests
and bannings are thought to be just as effective, and the
fear of international reactions. SACTU was driven underground due to the constant harassment by the state supported by the bourgeouisie.[46]

Like the legal trade unions' work, SACTU's activities were
very limited up until 1973. From this point onwards the
illegal organizations have probably also gradually gained
a foothold. Due to the character of its work it is naturally impossible to give statistics of membership etc. The
scope and strength of the organization can only be determined indirectly through, for example, the spreading of
illegal pamphlets or the arrests of SACTU activists.

D. Henson, who was legally occupied with organizing textile
workers, until he was banned in 1974, wrote later that
illegal organizations and strikes "are real phenomena in
working class action in South Africa."[47] In 1976 SACTU
stated that:

> "Despite this persecution, SACTU's work inside South
> Africa has in fact intensified, notably through the
> organization of factory committees." 48

The formation of committees and the distribution of illegal
information were given a priority in SACTU's work in the
1970's.

In 1979 SACTU activists (outside South Africa) criticised
the leadership for not doing enough to support the illegal
network in South Africa. As an outside observer it is not
possible to evaluate this criticism. In 1980 the question
of how the workers can best organize themselves illegally
has, however, had a prominent position in SACTU's paper,
'Workers' Unity'. On the whole, the size and strength of
the illegal organizations will become evident when legal
organizations are rendered impossible, and, consequently,
the trade union struggle will be forced to take solely
illegal forms.

At present SACTU activists are - in addition to building
an illegal network - trying to work inside the legal trade

unions, and thereby influencing their line of action. In an interview in 1981, Thozamila Botha, a former worker and community organization leader, publically stated:

> "On the whole SACTU is stronger in the independent and nonregistered trade unions, but within progressive unions, attached to other union bodies, SACTU-members can also be found." 49

There is no doubt that many of the independent trade unions have the same conception of the trade union struggle as SACTU. On the question of illegal versus legal organization SACTU stated in 1977 that:

> "Bitter experience has taught our people to use open form of organization, but not to rely on them, for they are fragile and easily attacked." 50

SACTU further added:

> "Organization on all possible levels is vital in the development of the fighting strength of the workers, to meet the great challenges which lie ahead. In the day to day battles for higher wages, better working conditions and trade union rights, the organization and consciousness of the workers is advanced." 51

Even though there are many reformists, opportunists, even collaborators in the legal trade unions, there are, according to SACTU:

> "... also many who walk a tight rope of personal danger in truly serving the struggle of the working class."

Even though the legal trade unions must, on the whole, keep their distance from the actual freedom struggle SACTU on the other hand seeks closer ties with them:

> "Our policy is to fight for independent unions and to give these new organizations our support - in so far as they advance the workers' struggle." (Emphasis is mine, jh). 52

This qualified support to the legal trade unions does not, however, prevent SACTU from attacking the legal trade unions' policy if SACTU considers such policy detrimental to the workers' struggle, for example, the economistic course followed by the TUCSA trade unions.

The state utilizes its repressive apparatus in an attempt to destroy SACTU. In 1977 two leading SACTU members were tortured to death by the security police, five were sentenced to life imprisonment, and four to between 7 and 18 years in prison. In the autumn of 1980 Oscar Mpeta, 71 years of age and one of the founders of SACTU, was charged

as an accomplice in the killing of two whites in the
summer of 1980. In the autumn 1981 when this is written
the trial still continued. During recent years Mpeta has been
legally employed at the African Food & Canning Workers Union
in Cape Town.

As to SACTU's relationship to the armed liberation struggle it was, as mentioned earlier, co-signatory to the Freedom Charter already in 1955 and has always recognized the
African National Congress (ANC) as the leading political
organization for the oppressed. If a person becomes a
member of SACTU, he/she will almost automatically be a
member of the ANC. Nevertheless, SACTU emphasizes the importance of an organized black working class in the process
of change:

> "Trade unions are only one form of organization re-
> quired by the workers in this great struggle for
> emancipation, but they are a vital and indispensable
> weapon in advancing this struggle." 53

SACTU stated elsewhere, that it is:

> "... important for them (the black workers, jh) as
> workers to participate fully in the liberation move-
> ment." 54

In the early sixties SACTU was accused of being a channel
for recruitment to the liberation struggle, whose major
role was to send people to military training in ANC's
exile-department. If this has ever been SACTU's policy, it
certainly has not played this role in the 1970's and 1980's.

It is essential to point out how SACTU stresses the
workers' participation in the political struggle - as
workers - due to their position in society as an exploited
class that at the same time constitutes the back-bone of
the South African economy. This is contrary to a nation-
alistic understanding of the situation where the workers
are conceived as ordinary citizens struggling for national
liberation.

Nevertheless, SACTU has been criticized for not conveying
a clear enough socialist consciousness of the situation,
and for not clearly putting forward demands that trans-
gress the framework of the capitalist society.[55] It is
also probable that there are different conceptions within
the organization itself in determining the position of the
anti-capitalist struggle in the present phase in relation
to the struggle for national liberation and basic demo-

cratic reforms. It appears that the latter type of demands
are most dominant in the 'Workers Unity', but I am not
certain if this is representative of SACTU's total spectrum
of activities.

3.8 CONCLUDING REMARKS

In relation to my earlier theoretical discussion it is
correct to say that a black organized labour force has
developed since around 1973, and has from the beginning of
the 1980's constituted a relatively permanent and independent structure with a substantial influence on society.
It is the strongest, legal and organized expression of the
dominated classes' desire to change the existing order of
society. Even though the organized labour force constitutes
a relatively small percentage of the total,[56] when compared
with certain European countries it nevertheless must be
perceived as a rather high percentage if the restrictive
conditions for their formation are taken under consider-
ation (25 % unemployed, repression, compound-system in
mining, etc.).

As to the connection between the organized and non-organized class-practice the Durban strikes illustrated this by
forming the basis of much trade union work in the 1970's.

The actual developments also illustrate the close connec-
tions between society's social structure, and the form and
content of the trade union movement. SACTU, for example,
takes up political questions because trade unions have so
many times before been persecuted by the state in order to
preserve the fundamental structures of a society, which
rests on the extreme exploitation of the black workers.
Since SACTU was not able to challenge the structures of
society, it had no other choice but to continue illegally,
if it intended to follow its original line of action.
Another example is the legal trade unions, who were forced
to keep a relatively low political profile in the middle
of the 1970's, because their position in relation to the
state's repressive structures was very weak after over ten
years of relatively successful bourgeois offensive against
the dominated classes.

As to the possibilities of transcending the economistic
line and taking up political questions the struggle does

nevertheless leave some space for political action for the legal trade unions, and this space increases in tempo with the black trade unions' constant and increasingly stronger position in society. The degree of freedom that arises here, is utilized by the trade unions in different ways. The ·TUCSA affiliated unions are subjected to political pressure for TUCSA not to challenge the existing structure of society. CUSA trade unions have a greater degree of independence, but in theory and practice they make a distinction between trade union and political work, and they generally perceive their own efforts as 'apolitical work', which is primarily concerned with attaining better wages and working conditions. The independent progressive trade unions and to some extent FOSATU, have on the other hand transgressed the economism (or 'trade-unionism') and maintained their right to involve in the political areas that their members find relevant.

As representatives of the exploited and oppressed working class they also insist on their right to demand more fundamental changes in the structure of society. SACTU is then able to more precisely define these basic changes without the risk of being crushed due to its illegal status. SACTU, at the same time, is seeking to combine the long-term goal with the immediate demands for better wages and working conditions.

It is obvious that there in principle is no contradiction between the legal and illegal struggle. If the goal is to maximize the dominated classes' position of strength, then parts of the legal and the illegal struggle supplement each other. At the same time, it appears that, for example, the TUCSA-affiliated unions' line of approach is an obstacle to the strengthening of black workers' influence on historical change.

Notes

1 See, for example, M. Lacey: Working for Boroko. The Origins of a Coersive Labour System in South Africa, Johannesburg 1981. Luckhardt/Wall: Organize or Starve, the History of the South African Congress of Trade Unions, London 1980. Feit: Workers without Weapons, Hamden, 1975. Horrel: South African Trade Unionism, Johannesburg, 1961. Horrel: South Africa's Workers. Their Organizations and Patterns of Employment, Johannesburg, 1969. Lewis: African Trade Unions and the South

African State, 1947-53, dupl. Cape Town 1976. A History of Workers Organizations, IIE, Durban 1977 (The Worker Handbook no. 1) The History of Labour Organization in South Africa, FOSATU (Phil Bonner), 1979/80. Haarløv/ Schmidt: The political Development in South Africa in the 1970's - with particular emphasis on the conditions on the black labour market (Historisk-Fagligt Appendix) København, 1979: (In Danish). Webster (ed.): Southern African Labour History, Johannesburg, 1978. Callinicos: Gold and Workers 1886-1924 - A People's History of South Africa, Vol. 1, Johannesburg 1980.

2   The special conditions within the mining & agricultural sector will not be taken up in this report.

3   Grobbelaar: The Parallel Trade Union, TUCSA, 1974. Quoted from J. Lewsen: "The role of Registered Trade Unions in the Black Trade Union Movement, South African Labour Bulletin, 3, 4, 1977, p. 49.

4   FOSATU: The Parallel Union Thrust, Memorandum, Nov. 8, 1979.

5   Work in Progress, 18, p. 59.

6   South African Labour Bulletin, March, 5, 1979, p. 98 ('The National Union of Clothing Workers, Interview with: Mrs. Lucy Mvubelo, Secretary General').

7   Ibid. p. 98.

8   Natal Mercury, April 23, 1975. Quoted from D. Davis: "African Trade Unions at the Crossroad", African Communist, 64, 1976, p. 101.

9   Star, Johannesburg, Nov. 9, 1974.

10 L. Mvubelo: Black South African Trade Unionist Looks at the Role of American Companies in South Africa, California, 1980, pp. 9 & 14.

11 D. Hemson; 'Trade Unionism and the Struggle for Liberation in South Africa.' ,Capital & Class, 6, 1978, p. 32.

12 This figure covers over 45,378 signed-up members and 13,914 paid up members in April 1981, according to "CUSA-Membership Statistics between April 1980 and April 1981". I.e. only 30,6 % of the members are up to date in their payments, while the rest are more than 3 months behind. Even though there is always a certain percentage of the workers in arrears in their union dues in South Africa, it is nevertheless a very high percentage, (more than 2/3 of the members). In April 1980, 1/4 of FOSATU's members were more than 3 months in arrears.

    In regard to CUSA's "membership Statistics" it is questionable as to what extent Commercial Catering & Allied Workers Union of South Africa (CCAWUSA) can be included among its members, for the Secretary General of CCAWUSA stated in 1981 that they did not consider themselves as one of CUSA's members. In April 1981 CCAWUSA had 10,000 signed up members of which 4,400 were up to date in their dues. Politically CCAWUSA is more in accordance with the independent trade unions than with the other CUSA-unions.

13 UTP - Report - 1976, pp. 2, 28 & 32.

14 See Labour News, ICFTU, African Regional Organization, vol. 60-61, Feb. 1981, p. 6.

15 'Council of Unions of South Africa', mimeo CUSA, 1981, p. 6.

16 'Policy Document on some Issues', mimeo CUSA, 1981, p. 2.

17 Both the number of affiliated unions and the total number of members (the 50,000 are signed members) are approximate figures, because merges occur as do break-offs.

18 FOSATU Constitution, 1979 Congress Resolution 8, p. 55.

19 Ibid. 3.12, p. 20.

20 Ibid. Congress Resolution 7, p. 55.

21 Mark Loft: Interview with Alec Erwin, July, 1980 (tape).

22 FOSATU Report April 1979 - April 1980, p. 9.

23 Financial Mail, Sept. 11, 1981.

24 The figures in parenthesis specify the number of signed up members in 1981. Similar to the FOSATU affiliated unions there are probably around 1/4 of the members who are in arrears in their union dues. The whole statistical overview must be taken with some reservation, because these unions are a long way from becoming firmly established in regard to the recruitment of new members or the geographical expansion of the organizations. (See also Appendix 2 for further information).

Please notice that I did not mention the Media Workers Association of South Africa, MWASA. The social distance between its members and the black working class is so great that it would be incorrect to deal with them on the same level as the rest of the trade unions. In addition, MWASA is the only independent union which still follows what can be characterized as a Black Consciousness line, that is to say, race is given a priority position rather than class relations.

In the middle of 1981 the Black Municipal Workers Union definitively broke with the Black Consciousness influence on the trade union (this is why they will probably operate under another name in future). The Black Allied Workers Union which was relatively active in the middle of the 1970's has no significance in the beginning of the 1980's.

25 In 1973, GWU started as an 'advice-service' for the black workers, but it gradually developed into an 'umbrella-organ' for a trade union structure, based on factory-committees. In the beginning it was called the Western Province Workers' Advice Bureau. In 1979 the name was changed to Western Province General Workers' Union and in 1981 the 'Western Province' was dropped because the organization tried to expand on a national level, especially among the dock workers.

26 Work in Progress, April 17, 1981, p. 6.

27 'Western Province General Workers' Union: Comment on the Question of Registration', South African Labour Bulletin, April 5, 1979, p. 120 f.

28 See Work in Progress, Feb. 16, 1981, p. 49, or 'Working for Ford?' in South African Labour Bulletin, 6, 2 & 3, 1980.

29 SASPU National, February 1981.

30 SASPU National, April (2, 4) 1981.

31 'Statement', August 1981.

32 Western Province General Workers' Union: 'Submission to the Department of Labour with regard to the proposed Industrial Conciliation Amendment Bill', April 19, 1981, p. 3.

33 SASPU National April (2, 4) 1981.

34 South African Allied Workers Union, 'Constitution', p. 1.

35 SASPU National, August (2, 6) 1981.

36 SASPU National, April (2, 4) 1981. Nelson Mandela is the leader of the illegal liberation movement, the African National Congress, ANC.

37 Western Province General Workers Union, op. cit., p. 121.

38 Financial Mail, Feb. 2, 1981 and SASPU National, Feb. 1981.

39 Work in Progress, April 1981, p. 7.

40 Evening Post/P.E. Herald (Port Elizabeth, July 15, 1981.

41 In the 1940's, CNETU functioned as an 'umbrella-organ' for over 150,000 workers, but its following was drastically reduced, primarily because of state-repression. See note 24 for material on CNETU.

42 SACTU: Workers' Struggle for Freedom, 1976, p. 14.

43 Ibid., p. 10.

44 Ibid., p. 19.

45 Horrel: South Africa's Workers, p. 26.

46 In Feit's "Workers without Weapons" (pp. 162-172) it was maintained that SACTU in the beginning of the 1960's functioned as a cover for ANC and Communist parties' illegal activities, and that SACTU played a major role in recruiting people for military training outside the country's border. I am unfortunately not able to test the validity of this.

47 Hemson, op. cit., p. 23.

48 SACTU: Workers in Chains, London 1976, p. 17.

49 Africa-Bulletin, no. 59, 4/1981 (Stockholm) (My translation from Swedish, jh.)

50 Workers Unity, 6, 1977, p. 3.

51 J. Gaetsewe: 'Trade Unions and the Struggle for Liberation in South Africa' Notes and Documents, U.N., June, 1977, p. 8.

52 Workers' Unity, 5, 1977.

53 J. Gaetsewe, op. cit., p. 9.

54 Sechaba, 12, 1978, p. 17.

55 See The Workers' Movement and SACTU. A Struggle for Marxist Policies, London, 1979.

56 In South Africa the members of black trade unions constitute approximately 10 % of the black workers employed in manufacturing industry and about 2-3 % of the total black work force. The level of organization in Western Europe varies from around 25 % to 75 % of the work force.

4. LABOUR MARKET REGULATION

4.1 INTRODUCTION

In the beginning of the 1970's the Bantu Labour (Settlement of Disputes) Act (1953) and certain provisions of the Industrial Conciliation Act (1956) were the basis by which the state attempted to regulate the black workers' position on the labour market. The main provisions of this legislation were:

- a refusal to recognize black trade unions as a bargaining party in regard to wage and working conditions of the blacks.

- that the wages of the black workers were determined by the Industrial Councils (IC), where only white, coloured, and Indian trade unions, employers and the state were represented. In regions where there were no ICs, wages were determined by a state appointed 'Wage Board', or arbitrarily by the employers.

- that white, coloured and Indian trade unions were not allowed to have black members if they wanted to be registered; i.e. get the right to negotiate wages etc. in the Industrial Councils.

- the establishment of a conciliation system for black workers which consisted of 'Works Committees' in the factories, 'Regional Bantu Labour Councils' (RBLC) and a 'Central Bantu Labour Board' (CBLB). There were no representatives from the black workers in RBLC or CBLB, and in 1973 only 24 Works Committees had been formed.

- an introduction of legal job-reservation in industry.

These provisions represent the repressive line against the black workers. They deprive black workers of any form of infuence on their wage and working conditions.

It is this legislation which the Durban strikers of 1973 attacked. The central problems for both the government and the employers were partly that the widespread strikes caught them unawares, partly that they lacked proper communication channels for negotiating a solution with the striking workers.

4.2 THE 1973 ACT

The government's response came in 1973, with the Bantu Labour Relations Regulation Amendment Act, which focused particularly on one point: the improvement of each individual employers' communication network with their employers. The means to accomplish this was the establishment of Works and Liaison Committees. In the Liaison Committees, one half of the members were selected from the employers' staff and the other half from the workers. Works Committees consisted exclusively of workers. Liaison Committees were given first priority, since Works Committees could not be established in an industry where Liaison Committees already existed, while the opposite was not the case. Liaison Committees' function was exclusively consultative, and the manager's power was further increased because it was stipulated that management select the committee's chairman. Works Committees' function were to communicate the employees' demands to the employers and represent the employees in any eventual negotiation with the employers. If a Works Committee actually made an agreement with the employer there was for many reasons no way to enforce it. Firstly, it was very seldom that Works Committees had rules or regulations to follow and therefore agreements had no legal sanction. Secondly, a court verdict in 1976 deprived Works Committees of the right to take part in a trial. This meant that each worker had to conduct his or her case individually. Furthermore a Works Committee agreement covered only one workshop or factory and a Works Committee did not have members it was responsible to, nor an independent economic basis. Formally, the committee members had some protection against sacking workers on political grounds, but in reality, victimization of committee members was rather the rule than the exception.[2]

The employers clearly prefered LCs. An investigation in 1976[3] revealed that in 91 % of the cases the employers took the initiative in establishing Liaison Committees. In August 1977, 2,503 Liaison Committees and only 301 Works Committees had been established. In 1973 there were six Liaison Committees for every Works Committee. In 1977 the ratio was 8:1.

Apart from the committees there were three important elements in the 1973 AL. Firstly, it became possible for the Regional Bantu Labour Committees (RBLC) to admit black members from Works or Liaison Committees within a particular branch or industry, when problems within this branch were discussed. Likewise, the Chairman of RBLC was permitted to have an African committee member participate in discussions in the Industrial Councils, though without voting rights.

A second important element of the 1973 act was the introduction of 'Wage Orders'. This meant that a representative group of employers could present the Minister of Labour with a proposal for a given fixed wage within their area or region. The Minister of Labour (now called M. o. Manpower) could then make the proposal compulsory for that region. In other words, a wage-level could be set without any influence at all from the black workers. In 1975, 13 Wage Orders were issued which covered well over 100,000 workers.[4]

The third element concerned the right to strike. The black workers were formally given the right to strike. The extent of this was, however, limited. Many industries - the so-called essential services - were not included, and where there were Industrial Council agreements, Wage Board determination or Wage Orders, strikes were also forbidden. Furthermore, before a strike was considered legal it was necessary for the parties involved to go through a very complicated process of arbitration. Added to this, the right to strike was not - as it was the case for the registered trade unions - a part of a mutually accepted conciliation system. Lastly black workers were still punished much more severely than other races for illegal strikes. Until the beginning of the 1980's only one strike - out of thousands - was formally legal.

In relation to the central problem discussed in this research report, it is obvious that the Liaison Committees, the Wage Order system, and the illusory right to strike represent a continuation of the repressive line against the black workers. It is questionable whether the establishment of Works Committees and the participation in RBLC and the Industrial Councils are an indication that the system is opening up. But the fact that the law and the employers gave first priority to Liaison Committees does not point in the direction of real change being carried out, and the formal participation in the RBLC & Industrial Councils becomes insignificant, because all the influence there remains with the others who traditionally have done everything to hold the black workers down.

In spite of the repressive content of the law some of the trade unions have tried to use Works Committees in their work. They got their people elected to the committees, and because the committee members constituted a part of the whole labour struggle Works Committees could become a useful instrument for the workers. But this was surely not the government's or the employers' intention for the committees. It was the employers who pressed for the Liaison Committees' priority position in the Act, and the government's aim was to render the black trade unions superfluous by establishing the committee system. The Minister of Labour stated in his presentation of the law in 1973:

> "I think that the establishment of these Works Committees will really deprive these Bantu trade unions ... of their life blood and necessity for existence." 5

The background of this was, according to the Minister of Labour:

> "On the basis of experience gained in this country in the past, and the way in which these (Bantu trade unions, jh) were also applied as political instruments it is not in the interest of South Africa that Bantu trade unions should be recognized." 6

To summarize, the dominant classes in 1973 went wholeheartedly in for a continued, but more flexible repressive line. This does not imply an attempt of co-optation, because the blacks are not permitted a platform within the existing system's framework. Attempts are constantly being made to keep black workers organizations outside the system, to fragment them, in order to prevent them from building up a class organization that could threaten the prevailing order.

4.3 CHANGES IN LABOUR MARKET REGULATION IN 1977

The Bantu Labour Relations Regulations Amendment Act that was passed in 1977, contains only minor adjustments in relation to the law of 1973, and affirms a continuation of the repressive course. The purpose of the changes was to strengthen liaison at the expense of Works Committees, and, to a certain extent, deracialize the RBLC and the Central Bantu Labour Board (CBLB). In addition to this, the Liaison and Works Committee members were bound to an oath of secrecy.

The genesis of the law is, however, more interesting than its content. Already in 1975 the government laid the ground for a new legislation. The background was the ineffectiveness of the law of 1973, which was not capable of making the new trade unions redundant, nor of stopping the strike-wave among the African workers. The government's proposal in 1975 was an attempt to get the committee system to function by abolishing the privileged position of Liaison Committees and giving the committees a greater influence in wage negotiations. The committees could form an "Industrial Committee", but only within their branch of industry. The committee could, without the right to vote, participate in Industrial Councils' meetings, and if there were no Industrial Councils in the area or region, the committee could negotiate wages with the RBLC and the employers. All Industrial Committee-members should, however, be permanently employed, and they had no organization behind them or economic basis, much less the right to call the workers on strike legally.

I will interpret this as a co-optive attempt, since a proportion of the dominated classes are given a platform with a certain formal influence, without in reality allowing them to increase their position of strength in society.

These tendencies towards co-optation were not carried through, as mentioned earlier. The 1975 proposal was scrapped after very strong protests from the right-wing white trade unions and the combined efforts of the employers, especially the Afrikaanse Handelsinstitut, which feared that the Industrial Committees and the strengthening of the position of the Works Committees would pave the way for black workers to attain legitimate trade union rights. But this was not the government's intention either. The fact that the government was against the black workers having any form of labour rights in 1977 was illustrated by the banning of even moderate trade union leaders.[7]

As to opposition from the employers' side, there might be two different reasons why they were afraid of the economic and political potential of a strong and well organized black trade union movement. Firstly, employers might believe that the trade unions would invariably be used in a revolutionary movement that would lead to the nationalization of private property, and deprive the existing owners of their economic basis for existence.

Secondly, the employers might believe that the trade unions would be used to bring about economic improvements and political reforms, for example, one man one vote, within the framework of the capitalist market system. If this is the main reason why the employers are against the recognition of trade unions, it indicates that they are materially dependent on the state's repressive apparatus and the present political distribution of power, which ensures them a very cheap labour force.

Under all circumstances, if the employers must agree on the recognition of the black trade unions, then they will try to make sure that the trade unions can not be used in an offensive political and economic struggle. More light is thrown on this question in the following discussion of the third reform of the labour market regulation in the 1970's: The Industrial Act of 1979, which was prepared on the basis of a report from the Wiehahn-Commission.

4.4 THE WIEHAHN COMMISSION AND THE INDUSTRIAL CONCILIATION AMENDMENT ACT OF 1979

The Wiehahn Commission was formed in 1977 in order to evaluate the then existing labour market legislation, and if necessary to recommend changes. The Commission consisted of representatives from registered trade unions and from industry together with economists.[8]

In May 1979 the Commission delivered a report which mainly dealt with the question of the scope and content of trade union rights, and in 1980 it finished another three reports dealing with 'Manpower Training', 'Employment & Social Security' and 'Health and Safety Conditions'. The following will center around the first report, because it focuses on the main theme of this research report. The content of the proposals, which only includes workers in the manufacturing industries, are as follows:

- Equal labour rights regardless of race. However, according to a large minority this should only be applied to blacks who have permanent residency in the White areas. Migrant workers are excluded.

- Trade Unions must be recognized by the Minister of Labour before any agreements with the employers can be considered legally binding.

- Trade unions are forbidden to participate in political activities.

- Trade unions must be subjected to financial control by the government, and the government can forbid them to carry out certain undesirable activities.

- 'Stop-order facilities', whereby employers withhold the union dues from the workers' wage are allowed, but only with the permission of the workers involved, and only to be utilized by registered trade unions.

- The method and content in teaching about labour market conditions must follow the lines laid down by the state, and institutions and trade unions that wish to hold courses on labour market conditions must first be approved by the Minister of Labour.

- "Job-reservation" shall be eliminated, but the involved White trade unions have the right of veto.

- "Closed-shop" agreements between the employers and the white trade unions, which protect the white workers' jobs are retained.

- The rights to veto in the Industrial Councils are introduced.

- The committee system is to be extended to include all workers, but the question of inter-racial committees must be decided locally.

- The committees have a right to negotiate but only in the regions not covered by the Industrial Council.

- An Industrial Court is to be established.

- A "National Manpower Commission" shall monitor the new labour market system's development, and regularly come with suggestions for improvements.

- The Minister of Labour shall approve racially integrated trade unions, and race-exclusive trade unions shall be protected.

- Provisions for equal pay for equal should be enforced.

- A job as an apprentice shall be open to all races, but this depends upon the acceptance of the white trade unions.

- Racially separate facilities in the industries shall be abolished.

The government published a 'White Paper' after the release of the Wiehahn report, outlining its own position. With a few exceptions the government accepted the major points in the report. The important difference was the question of the status of the migrant workers. The government agreed with the minority position that they could not become

members of registrered trade unions. Moreover, the guiding
rule should be that the trade unions should be 'racially
pure'. Racially mixed trade unions must have special permission from the Minister of Labour. In July 1979 a new
Industrial Conciliation Act was passed in Parliament. It
followed - with the modifications of the 'White Paper' -
the Wiehahn report's new model for the registration of
trade unions with black members, plus the establishment of
an Industrial Court and the National Manpower Commission.[9]

Migrant workers and foreign workers as a whole are to be
excluded from the system, because trade unions must not
have workers in this category as members, if they wish to
be registered unions. This provision excluded around half
of the African workers. This presented a serious problem
especially for the trade unions in the province of Natal,
where the townships for the black industrial workers are
often placed in Kwa-Zulu Bantustan, and in the Cape where
the majority of the African workers are migrant workers
from Transkei or Ciskei. Needless to say, this deprives
the trade unions of their most vital means of power: The
possible monopolization of the supply of manpower.

Whilst the attitude towards the remaining content of this
new law varied very much from one trade union to another,
almost all of the trade unions dealt with in this report
were unanimous in their criticism of this particular provision. Foreign countries also complained, and maintained
that the whole reform was without content because of this
provision. Confronted with this opposition, and probably
as an attempt to split the common front against the new
law, the Minister of Labour (Manpower) changed the provision in September 1979 so that only the workers from
foreign countries were forbidden from joining trade unions
(the independent Bantustans were not considered as foreign
in this case.)

No changes were made, however, in another highly controver-
sial provision in the law: the registered trade unions
were still forbidden to have any connection with a political party, or to support a political party economically.

The demand for legal depoliticization of the trade unions'
work was supported even by the most progressive section of
capital. In their proposal to the Commission the Anglo-
American demanded:

> "Strict control of trade unions to avoid misuse for political ends through legal requirements, as well as additional restrictions laid down by employers." 10

This demand was supported by TUCSA, which assured that the trade unions with black members:

> "... will not become subject to disruptive actions by any political social or economic extremists." 11

It has been maintained many times in the Wiehahn Commissions report that the un-registered trade unions have much more independence and freedom of action than the registered trade unions who are subjected to the Industrial Conciliation Act:

> "Black trade unions are subject neither to the protective and stabilizing elements of the system nor to its essential discipline and control. They in fact enjoy much greater freedom than registered unions, to the extent that they are free if they so wished to participate in politics and to utilize their funds for whatever purpose they see fit." (My emphasis, jh.) 12

This great freedom, however, is relative, for example, if one looks at the many bannings of trade union activists. Nevertheless, it is clear that the new proposal was an attempt to control the black trade unions' relatively independent growth. The background for this was the realization that the growth of the black trade unions couldn't be stopped by holding them outside of the system, and a direct prohibition against them would only strengthen the illegal labour struggle:

> "A prohibitation would undoubtedly have the effect of driving Black trade unionism underground and uniting Black workers not only against the authorities, but more important, also against the system of free enterprise in South Africa. It would certainly add fuel to the flames of radicalism on the part of those who wish to overthrow the system." (My emphasis, jh.) 13

Through such control-measures the government tried to encapsulate the black workers' offensive trade union struggle into an economistic one, and thereby twist the concessions so they, in fact, benefitted the existing system. This attempt to ensure that the trade unions did not, as class-organizations, form a basis for economic and political changes, has been a sine qua non for employer acceptance of the new legislation.

In addition to this, there was another major element in the Industrial Conciliation Amendment Act (ICAA) of 1979.

This was the scaling down of the job-reservation provisions in the legislation.[14]

I will try to relate these two central elements with the economic crisis, which was characterized by an increase in the mobilization of the dominated classes in the 1970's.

The economic crisis led to a fall in the rate of profit, and a decline in foreign investments. This caused the employers to press for a relative or absolute lowering of the wage-level for all categories of wage-labourers, and for an increase in the mechanization of industry. The white workers have traditionally monopolized the skilled-labour jobs, and because of the relative scarcity of manpower they have been able to attain relatively high salaries. The substitution of the expensive white skilled workers by machinery and cheap black manpower started already in the boom period in the 1960's and the early part of the 1970's. The white workers were bought out of their jobs by 'promoting' them to company officials, such as control and supervision positions, or they got other privileges (This is called the floating-colour-bar). Harry Oppenheimer of Anglo-American stated that:

> "We are in a position that we can maintain this system, and allow the whole structure to float upward so that everybody benefits." 15

But during the economic crisis the financial basis for such a course was lacking. The Chairman of the Federal Chamber of Industries stated in 1976 that:

> "Present policy was forcing employers to pay artificial premium wages (to the white workers, jh.), and thereby increasing instead of reducing costs."

This was under the given conditions:

> "seriously affecting South Africa's capacity to compete on international markets." 16

Whilst the need for educating and training the black labour force has been documented time and again since the 1960's, it was the economic (and political) crisis at the end of the 1970's that forced the employers to break the white workers' monopoly on certain jobs. It was necessary to open up for cheap black manpower, in order to eliminate the artificial scarcity of skilled workers.

As mentioned earlier, the economic crisis also led to an attempt by the employers to lower the black worker's real wage. This implies a need to control the trade unions' defense of their members' wage and working conditions. The employers wanted a co-optative trade union leadership that would not actively participate in the struggle to preserve and possibly increase the members' real wage. The employers wanted the labour leaders to convince its members that they had a common interest with the employers in blocking wage-rises. It was hoped that this type of leadership would be created by the new legislation.

In regard to the political crisis, the ICAA tried to contribute to the stabilization of the situation in two ways. Firstly, the removal of the legal job-reservation provision was part of the attempt to create a black middle class.[17] According to Rob Davies, the removal of the job-reservation would lead to a middle class that would constitute between 4 and 10 % of the economically active proportion of the African population in 1990 as against 3 % in 1979.[18]

The development of an African middle class is intended to form a 'buffer-zone' between the bourgeoisie and the black working class, and thereby prevent the formation of a common front against the existing system. The Riekert Commission Report and the laws it has given rise to, supplement in this connection the reforms of the Wiehahn Commission. The essence of the Riekert Commission's proposal is to split the black working class on two fronts. Firstly between the black permanent residents in the townships in the white areas on the one side, and the migrant workers and the unemployed in the Bantustans on the other. For example, it is proposed that the fine for employing illegal black workers in the white areas be drastically raised, and the blacks with permanent residency in the white areas shall be given more freedom to seek jobs where they want to. Secondly, the Riekert Commission's proposal is designed to break the common front among the township residents by offering the better-off a possiblity for semi-home owner-ship-loans to build houses etc.

Turning back to the ICAA - the other way it tried to stabilize the political situation was through the attempt to build up a co-optative leadership in the trade unions, which would deprive them of the potential political power

they have as a class-organization , and confine the workers' struggle to an economism, which questions neither
the system's political nor economic framework.

The major activity of this type of labour movement would
be to negotiate in the Industrial Councils on the distribution of possible improvements in productivity.

All in all the ICAA represented a deviation from the
repressive line's total dominance. The repression was
supplemented with the strategy of co-optation. It was not
a democratization, because the purpose of the many control-
institutions was precisely to prevent the trade unions
from developing into a real power base, which could
strengthen the workers' postion.

Has ICAA fulfilled its purpose in the two years it has
existed? In regard to the job-reservation arrangement there
is no doubt that the abolition of nearly all of the
legally stipulated rules has gradually promoted the liquida-
tion of the other job-reservation agreements, too. These
often took the form of a closed-shop agreement between the
white trade unions and the employers. The economic situation has, however, changed. The general economic upswing
in 1979/80 in South Africa, due to the increase in the
price of gold has on the one side made it of less importance for the employers to abolish the whites' monopoly of
certain jobs on the basis of the high economic costs. On
the other side, the 'boom' underlined the serious shortage
of skilled workers, and at the same time, in the beginning
of the 1980's the white workers were probably not in a
strong enough position to prevent the abolition of the
job-reservation agreements and the starting of vocational
training for blacks.

Even though blacks are climbing up the job-hierarchy to an
increasing degree, this has not assumed the dimensions
that could form the basis for an independent social force,
that would be able to constitute a moderate force in
society's development. In addition, there is nothing to
substantiate that a black middle class would support the
existing order. Is it not more likely that they would ally
themselves with an offensive black working class than with
a system, that contains a national oppression of the black
population? Also, the new labour legislation did not lead
to a situation where a co-optative leadership in the trade

unions prevented militant wage-struggles. On the contrary, the year 1980 experienced, as we have seen, the second largest number of strikes since the Second World War.

Nor has the government succeeded in checking the trade union's involvement in politics. It is precisely those trade unions that have a pronounced political profile that have experienced the largest growth in the period after the introduction of the ICAA.

As to the employers' reaction to the ICAA they - initially - adopted a very uncompromising attitude towards trade unions that were critical of ICAA. In section 3.3 it was shown how they actively tried to encourage the TUCSA-affiliated unions to out-maneouvre the other trade unions. Often they would only negotiate with trade unions that were regis- tered, or in the least had applied for registration, and/or were willing to join an Industrial Council.[19]

Faced with constant strike activities and the growth of the trade unions that rejected the law, they could not maintain a united front. One side steadfastedly supported the restrictive line. They refused to deal with non-regis- tered trade unions and replaced the whole labour force if they went on strike. On the other side some of the employers maintained from 1980/81 and onwards that what was crucial for them was to what degree the trade unions represented the work force, and not primarily the question of whether they were registered or not. This group of employers consists of rather large industries, for example, Barlow Rand, Ford, plus the Federated Chamber of Industries.

4.5 THE 1981 REVISION

The government's reaction came in the spring of 1981 in the form of a proposal for changes in the ICAA, the Industrial Conciliation Draft Amendment Bill. The main content was:

- that the prohibition against being connected to a politi- cal party was extended to include any form of support to or influence on the members' attitude, which would be advantageous for a political organization. This provision was also valid for non-registered unions;
- that the registration authorities were given the author- ity to administratively dissolve the existing registered trade unions. The authorities were not obliged to give any reason for such a step;

- that strike-ballots should be controlled;
- that support to illegal strikes should be forbidden;
- that it should be forbidden for employers to give stop-order facilities to non-registered trade unions, whilst they should be obliged to render this service to the registered trade unions;
- that all references to race and sex discrimination should be removed from the law.

At approximately the same time the government came with another legal proposal - Manpower Training Bill. According to this Bill, non-registered trade unions are only to be allowed to carry out courses for their members on labour market conditions at registered course centres, and all courses must be approved by the authorities. Registered trade unions may decide themselves whether their training centres should be registered or not.

These proposals are similar to ICAA's in that there is a mixture of limited reforms and an extension of control. Partly they can just be seen as a part of the gradual implementation of the Wiehahn-Commission's proposals. Partly they can be perceived as an attempt to put pressure on the non-registered trade unions to make them join the new system. This was expressed in the proposals where they tried to hamper the non-registered trade unions' work. The extended prohibition against political activities was to prevent them from working together with community organizations, the prohibition to support strikes should weaken the members' actions, and the deprivation of the stop-order facilities was an attempt to choke the trade unions economically.

The proposals were met with strong criticism from all sides. FOSATU threatened to withdraw its application for registration, and the independent trade unions strongly protested. The Federated Chamber of Industries stated that what was important was to make the idea of being registered more attractive, and CUSA protested against the control of non-registered trade unions. Even TUCSA was against the Draft Bill. TUCSA felt that the commitment to give stop-order facilities to the registered trade unions was of too much help to the newly registered black trade unions, and TUCSA was also against the authorities' right to dissolve registered trade unions and their control of strike-ballots.

In August 1981 the government then presented the revised
Industrial Amendment Bill to Parliament. The Bill complied
with all of TUCSA's objectives and in addition, retained
the provision of 1979 against any connection or support to
a political party.

A new feature was that the prohibition should also apply
to non-registered trade unions. In addition, the government
reintroduced, under pressure from the Afrikaanse Handelsinstitut, a committee-system in the industries in the form
of work-councils; i.e. multiracial liaison committees.[20]
All in all the attempt to extend control of the non-registered trade unions was retained, while the degree of control over the registered trade unions remained unchanged.

It did not take long for the trade unions to react.
Already on the 8th of August 1981 a joint meeting was held
in Cape Town. Over 100 representatives from 29 CUSA, FOSATU
and independent trade unions participated. It was agreed
that they would not conform to the prohibition against
supporting their members on strike, and furthermore they
rejected the system of registration "insofar as it is
designed to control and interfere in the internal affairs
of unions".[21] They also rejected the idea that the system
of Industrial Councils was an acceptable way of solving
problems, and urged trade unions that had not joined the
Industrial Councils to remain outside. It was also agreed
upon to establish joint solidarity-committees in the individual regions. They should first deal with the question
concerning the authorities' encroachment on the union
leaders and activists.

The meeting in Cape Town was a historical one. Firstly, in
itself it was an achievement to bring the frequently con-
flicting trade unions together. Secondly, the meeting was
the first collective debate on the central problems concerning the labour market since the upswing in union activities in the beginning of the 1970's. Thirdly, the joint-
document was characterized by its radical content. Finally,
this meeting contained the germ for a larger collaboration
between the trade unions in future, but probably only on
an ad hoc basis in the short run.

The Federated Chamber of Industries (FCI) also sent out a new statement in August 1981 on labour market conditions.[22] In regard to the registration process FCI urged the government "to make it a neutral one". As regard wage-fixing by the Industrial Councils the FCI felt that the act should be supplemented with decentralized agreements between trade unions and employers at each individual factory. Moreover, the FCI wanted the state to remain neutral in relation to the parties involved in the labour market "avoiding as far as possible bannings and detention under security legislation". Without directly criticising the new proposal this declaration was clearly a dissociation from the general line emphasized in the proposal.

In the same resolution the FCI criticised employers who persecute the workers' representatives and who create conditions that lead to intervention by the authorities. According to the FCI, structures should be created in the industries that are "mutually acceptable to management and unions". This confirms indirectly the dissension among the employers in their attitude towards the trade unions.

In short, the situation is very unstable. The government will pass a Bill which is an extension of a legislation that has failed to function as it was intended, and which in advance is certain to be met with very strong protests.

It is possible that the government will create conditions that will force the existing non-registered trade unions to register, but the chance that this will check their radical and militant course of action is highly unlikely. As the situation stands now, this seems only possible through a total prohibition against trade unions or the imprisonment of their leaders etc. But this, according to the Wiehahn report, would only reinforce the illegal work and advance the anti-free enterprise line in the trade union struggle. Furthermore, this would deprive the employers of their channels of communication with the more and more self-confident and militant black workers, and once and for all remove the credability of the government's assertion that striking changes are being made in the apartheid system.

Notes

1 J.M. Bloch: 'The Legislative Framework of Collective Bargaining in South Africa', London, 1977, p. 27 in R. Stares: Black Trade Unions in South Africa: The Responsibilities of British Companies, CCSA, London, 1977.

2 See for example R. Stares op.cit. or South African Labour Bulletin, 3, 1, 1976, pp. 5-22 & Barge et al.: The Case for South African Unions, NUSAS, 1977, pp. 40-43 & 52-56.

3 D. Horner: "African Labour Representation and the Draft Bill to Amend the Bantu Labour Relations Regulations Act (No. 48 of 1953)", South African Labour Bulletin, 9 and 10, 1976.

4 D. Davis: African Workers and Apartheid, IDAF, London, 1978, p. 23.

5 House of Assembly Debates, 1973, col. 8779. quotation from Barge et al, op.cit., p. 32.

6 House of Assembly Debates, col. 1071, quotation from The Durban Strikes, IIE, Durban, 1976, p. 109.

7 In November 16th, 1976 Loet Douwes Dekker and Eric & Jean Tyacke from the Urban Training Project were banned.

8 The Wiehahn Commissions official name was 'Commission of Inquiry into Labour Legislation'. Its members were:
   - Nicholas E. Wiehahn (chairman), Professor, University of South Africa.
   - F.J. van der Merwe, Professor in economics, Pretoria University.
   - E.P. Drummond, Managing director of Steel and Engineering Industries Federation of South Africa (SEIFSA).
   - C.W.H. du Toit, Federated Chamber of Industries (FCI).
   - T.I. Steenkamp, General Mining and Finance Corporation.
   - F.V. Sutton, Association of Chambers of Commerce of South Africa.
   - A.I. Niewoudt, President of South African Confederation of Labour.
   - J.A. Grobbelaar, General Secretary of Trade Union Council of South Africa (TUCSA)
   - C.P. Grobler, Railways Artisans Staff Association.
   - T.S. Neethling, Confederation of Metal and Building Unions.
   - N.J. Hechter, Department of Labour.
   - G. Munsook, Executive Committee member of South African Indian Council.
   - C.A. Botes, National Union of Furniture and Allied Workers.
   - B.N. Mokoatle, School of Business Leadership, University of South Africa.

9 Other suggestions made by the Wiehahn Commission are included in, for example, a recent Bill, the Manpower Training Bill (B. 60-'81), 1981 and the Labour Relations Amendment Bill (B. 59-'81), 1981. The former is an attempt to control the content of labour market educational courses, while the latter applies, among others, to the multi-racial committees in the factories.

10 Cape Times, May 30th, 1978, quotation from Workers' Unity, Jan. 1979.

11 Workers' Unity, Jan. 1979.

12 Report of the Commission of Inquiry into Labour Legislation, Part 1. (The Wiehahn Commission's Report), p. 18.

13 Ibid. p. 20.

14 Gradually, because job reservations within the mining
   and certain areas of the construction sectors were maintained, and because the white trade unions had veto
   rights in the Industrial Councils against the abolition
   of the 'private' job reservations clauses.

15 First/Steele/Gurney: The South African Connection,
   London, 1973, p. 66, quotation from Rob Davis: The
   Wiehahn Commission and the Restructuring of the Racial
   Division of Labour in South Africa, paper presented to
   the CSE Conference, Bradford, July 1978, p. 6.

16 Rand Daily Mail, Oct. 7th, 1976, quotation from Rob
   Davis, op.cit. p. 6.

17 The elimination of job reservations will primarily
   create an elite among the black workers, but traditionally in South Africa they are included in the term 'the
   black middle class'. The latter consists furthermore of
   a traditional petit bourgeois (mostly tradesman), and
   the new petit bourgeoisie (mostly office workers in
   government institutions and in larger industries).

18 Rob Davis, op. cit. p. 10 f.

19 See Steel and Engineering Industries Federation of South
   Africa (SEIFSA): 'Guidelines for SEIFSA Member Companies
   on the Development and Participation of Black Workers
   in the Metal and Engineering and Allied Industries',
   1979.

20 Financial Mail, Aug. 7th, 1981.

21 See Rand Daily Mail, Aug. 10th, 1981, or Work in Progress, 20, Oct. 1981, which brought the full text of
   the statement.

22 See Evening Post (Port Elizabeth) Aug. 9th, 1981.

5. CONCLUSION AND PERSPECTIVES

This research report has identified two central changes: One in the dominated and one in the dominant classes' behaviour on the labour market.

The mass strike in Durban in 1973 was the turning point in the black workers' struggle. A ten year period of defensiveness was transformed into an offensive which has ever since gained momentum. Mass strikes have been carried out in 1976 and 1980, minor strikes have been a constant feature and black trade unions membership has increased tenfold. From 1979 and onwards the most impressive growth rates have been attained by the legal black trade unions who have rejected the government's labour market legislations, and are determined to decide themselves to what degree they will become politically involved. Moreover, there are no indications that SACTU's illegal work and its influence on the legal trade unions has increased in the early eighties.

The change in the government's labour market policy originated from the Wiehahn Commission's suggestion in 1979. Their intention was to supplement the system of repression by co-opting parts of the black trade union movement by isolating the leaders in a bureaucratic conciliation system. This form of control would prevent the black trade unions from carrying out an offensive, economic, and political line of action. Democratic reforms are non-existent, because the new laws prevent the black trade unions from building an organized basic structure in the form of independent and democratically formed trade unions which would mean a real strengthening of their position in society.

Will the government succeed in stabilizing the situation and control the black workers' offensive position by a co-optative strategy? This is highly unlikely.

Firstly, this assumption is supported by experiences of the first two years of the new labour market policies. The black workers' offensive, economic, and political struggle has not ceased, and the joint meetings between the trade unions in August 1981, indicate that even though there are internal disagreements, they are developing towards a

common negative attitude in regard to the central elements
in the labour market regulation. Furthermore, the bourgeoisie is divided on the question of recognizing non-registered trade unions.

Secondly, it appears that the analysis of the mass strikes
and the black workers' trade union struggle supports the
hypotheses that were put forth in the introduction of the
report about how:
- the lack of a reformist tradition,
- the fact that isolation-effect is not reproduced on the
  political and judicial level,
- and the state's obvious support of capital
create the background for a system-transcending consciousness among the black workers.

To be more concrete, the blacks did not experience any
improvements in their standard of living during the boom
of 1980/81. Reforms have not been introduced that would
provide each individual, regardless of race, with an equal
say in the functions of the political system, and the
state has constantly intervened in the labour struggle on
behalf of the employers. The anti-system attitude is an
important factor behind the rejection of the co-optative
attempts and it indicates that the emphasis in the future
is likely to be placed on democratic or even socialist
demands.

Finally a third factor must be stressed. The measures of
control in the labour market legislation of 1979 and the
revision in 1981 reveal a clear tendency only to introduce
reforms that can totally be controlled by the government,
and consequently, can not satisfy or fulfil the demands
made by the black workers. 'Too little - too late' describes this reform syndrome quite well. It is an excellent
illustration of the earlier mentioned problems that totalitarian regimes have when they want to open up the systems;
after, for a long time, having excluded the dominated
classes from any influence. From all appearances the government, in the beginning of the 1980's, is faced with an
insolvable problem of choosing between one of two alter-
natives. On the one side, the government can choose to
hammer away at the trade unions who criticize the regulation of the labour market. This, however, would have a

severe 'boomerang' effect, in that this would strengthen the illegal radical trade union activities, deprive the employers of communication channels to their workers, and mean a fatal loss of credibility for the government.

On the other side, the government can, with minor modifications, maintain the present labour market regulation. This would probably mean a further politicization and radicalization of the trade unions, and frequent strikes for economic improvements and recognition of workers' organizations are likely to ensue.

Of course, the government has a third alternative, and that is to introduce sweeping democratic reforms, but this is highly unlikely. Large parts of agricultural and industrial capital would not be able to survive without the present economic and political protection.

Neither is mining capital presently willing to pay the price of switching over from migrant workers to a system with a permanent labour force. Added to this - the white middle class, petit bourgeoisie and the white working class are politically turning more and more to the right, because they fear competition from the blacks, and are generally scared of the consequences of majority rule for their way of life.

In the short run the government will most likely attempt to solve the problem by continuing to arrest, ban or utilize other methods of persecuting the trade union leaders who are against the co-optative model. Whether this will retard the trade unions' rapid growth is still uncertain, but there is some indication that a relatively large number of workers have acquired some knowledge of trade union work, so that they are able to take the place of the leaders who the authorities remove from their union duties.

It is also highly probable that the government will present several more or less sophisticated proposals that - with both carrot and stick - will try to control the trade unions.

To sum up, it wouldn't be unrealistic to assume that the government will follow a zig-zag course between repressing the black trade unions even more and diverse co-optative attempts, which, however, will hardly bring the situation under control.

In the medium- and long-term view, it is essential not to consider the situation as static. Even though the existing positions of strength within the bourgeoisie do not form the basis for a democratization, an intensification of the class struggle can lead to the reorganization of the power-bloc because the very foundations of the existing mode of production is threatened.

The prospects of a defeat in Namibia, mass strikes and the intensification of the armed liberation struggle in South Africa itself are conditions that could trigger off a process, where the representatives of the large industrial capital or a military regime would attempt to carry out some democratic reforms in alliance with a third force in the black population, perhaps, G. Buthelezi's Inkata-movement, at the expense of, for example, part of the white agrarian capital and the white petit bourgeoisie.

An important question is, however, whether such a process would not be tantamount to the beginning of a revolutionary change in South Africa?

APPENDIX

LIST OF TRADE UNIONS & TRADE UNION BODIES RELEVANT TO THIS RESEARCH REPORT

Parallel Unions that are members of Trade Union Council of South Africa (TUCSA) (1979)

1. Motor Industry Workers' Union of South Africa.
2. African Transport Workers' Union.
3. African Leather Workers' Union.
4. African Trunk & Box Workers' Union.
5. African Tobacco Workers' Union.
6. National Union of Clothing Workers.
7. Textile Workers' Union.
8. South African Bank Employees' Union.
9. National Union of Engineering Industrial & Allied Workers' Union.
10. Electrical & Allied Workers' Union of South Africa.

Source: The Parallel Union Thrust, Memorandum issued by Fosatu 8.11.1979, quoted from South African Labour Bulletin, 5, 6 & 7, 1980, p.87.

Council of Unions of South Africa (CUSA) (1981)

1. Building Construction & Allied Workers' Union
2. Commercial Catering & Allied Workers' Union (see however note 34).
3. Food, Beverage Workers' Union.
4. South African Laundry, Dry Cleaning & Dyeing Workers' Union.
5. South African Chemical Workers' Union.
6. Steel, Engineering & Allied Workers' Union.
7. Transport & Allied Workers' Union.
8. United African Motor Workers' Union.

Source: Council of Unions of South Africa: Membership Statistics Between April 1980 and April 1981.

Federation of South African Trade Unions (FOSATU) (1981)

1. Chemical Workers' Industrial Union.
2. Eastern Province Sweet Food and Allied Workers' Union.
3. Engineering and Allied Workers' Union.
4. Glass and Allied Workers' Union.
5. Jewellers & Goldsmiths' Union.
6. Metal and Allied Workers' Union.
7. National Union of Motor Assembly and Rubber Workers' Union.
8. National Union of Textile Workers.
9. Paper, Wood and Allied Workers' Union.
10. Sweet, Food and Allied Workers' Union.
11. Transport and General Workers' Union.
12. Tanning, Footwear and Allied Workers' Union.

Source: The author's own estimation.

The independent Trade Unions (1981)

1. General Workers' Union (1973/1981; see note 52) (Cape Town, Port Elizabeth, East London, Durban).*
2. Food & Canning Workers' Union/African Food & Canning Workers' Union (1941) (The whole country, but its main base is the Cape Province).
3. South African Allied Workers' Union. (1979) (East London, King Williams Town, Durban, Port Elizabeth, Johannesburg).
4. Motor Assembly & Component Workers' Union of South Africa (October 1980) (Port Elizabeth, Pretoria).
5. General Workers' Union of South Africa (April 1981) (Port Elizabeth).
6. Black Municipality Workers' Union (June 1980) (Johannesburg, but it will probably expand its activities to other areas as well).
7. General and Allied Workers' Union (July/August 1980) (Johannesburg/Reef-area).

* The first brackets indicate when the union was formed; the second, the area(s) where it has its strongest representation. This information has been included because of the very limited information that is generally available about these unions (for membership figures: see section 3.6).

Source: The author's own estimation.

REFERENCES

Aagaard/Possing: "Kommentar til artiklen: Betingelser for socialistisk fagforeningsarbejde." Kurasje, 11, 1975.

Adler, T. (ed.) Perspectives on South Africa. Witwatersrand, 1977.

African Food & Canning Workers' Union/Food & Canning Workers' Union:
Memorandum of objections ... regarding the Draft Industrial Conciliation Amendment Bill, 1981.
Handbook for Committee Members, n.d.,
Resolutions, n.d.,
Various Circular letters and Newsletters.

Ainslie, R.: Masters and Serfs, Farm Labour in South Africa. DAF, London, 1977.

Andersen, Heine: Notat om samfundsstruktur, organisationer og klassekampfelt, mimeo. April 1977.

BAWU:
Call to organize and form Black Trade Unions in South Africa, Johannesburg, n.d.,
Constitution, n.d.

Berge/Coleman/Edmon/van Heerden: The Case for South African Unions, NUSAS, 1977.

Berntson, L.: Politiska Partier och Sociala Klasser, Lund, 1974.

Bregnsbo, H.: Interessegrupper, Viborg, 1975.

Brooks/Birckhill: Whirlwind before the storm, London 1980.

Callinicos, Luli: Gold and Workers 1886-1924. A People's History of South Africa, Volume one, Johannesburg, 1980.

Callinicos/Rogers: Southern Africa after Soweto, Pluto Press, London 1977.

CDR-Seminar Papers, B 81.13., Papers Presented at the South Africa Seminar, 12th of September 1981, Copenhagen, 1981.

Christensen og Mortensen: "På vej mod en marxistisk fagforeningsteori", Häften för Kritiska Studier, 5, 1977.

Conditions of the Black Worker, Study project on external investment in South Africa and Namibia, Uppsala 1975.

Cooper, C. & Ensor, L.: PEBCO - a black mass movement, SAIRR, Johannesburg, 1981.

Council of Unions of South Africa (CUSA):
Introduction.
Policy Document on some Issues, mimeo, 1981.
Membership Statistics Between April 1980 and April 1981.

Davies, D.: African Workers and Apartheid, London, 1978.

Davies, D.: African Trade Unions - Reformist or Revolutionary?, African Communist, 3rd qtr. 62, 1975.

76

Davies, D.: African Unions at the Crossroads, African Communist, lst qtr., 1976.

Davies, k.: The Wiehahn Commission and the Restructuring of the Racial Division of Labour in South Africa, Paper presented to the CSE Conference, mimeo, Bradford, 1978.

Davies, R.: "The Class Character of South Africa's (Labour) Conciliation Legislation", South African Labour Bulletin, 2, 6, 1976.

Davies & Lewis: "Industrial Relations Legislation", Review of African Political Economy, 7, 1976.

Dekker, L.D. et al.: Case Studies in African Labour Action in South Africa and Namibia (S.W.A.), In Sandbrook/Cohen (ed.): Development of an African Working Class: Studies in Class formation and action, London 1975.

Department of Manpower: Labour Relations Amendment Bill, B. 59-81 + Explanatory Memorandum, W.P. 10-'81. Manpower Training Bill, 60-'81 + Explanatory Memo. W.P. Second Wage Amendment Bill. B. 62-'81. Guidance and Placement Bill. B. 61-'81 + Explanatory Memo. W.P. 8-'81.

Duncan, Sheena: The Central Institutions of South African Labour Exploitation, South African Labour Bulletin, 3, 9, 1977.

Erwin, A.: An Essay on Structural Unemployment, South African Labour Bulletin, 4, 3, 1978.

Erwin/Webster: Ideology and Capitalism in South Africa, in Schlemmer/Webster (ed.): Change, Reform and Economic Growth in South Africa, Johannesburg, 1978.

Federation of South African Trade Unions (FOSATU): FOSATU Report. April 1979 - April 1980. FOSATU WORKER NEWS; various issues.

Workers' Struggle at Colgate, issued by Chemical Workers' Industrial Union, 1981. Memorandum on the Proposed Amendments to the Industrial Conciliation Act, 1981. Health & Safety at Work, April 1980. To All Union Members. (2 newsletters from NUMARWOSA about MACWUSA) 1981. Datsun Workers (pamphlet from NUMARWOSA).

Feit, E.: Workers Without Weapons, The South African Congress of Trade Unions and the Organization of the African Workers, Hamden Connecticut, 1975.

First/Steele/Gurney: The South African Connection, London, 1972.

Gaetsewe,J,: Interview: The Role of the Workers in the South African Liberation Struggle, Sechaba, lst. qtr., 1978.

Gaetsewe, J.: Trade Unions and the Struggle for Liberation in South Africa, Centre Against Apartheid, Notes and Documents, 1977.

General and Allied Workers' Union (GAWU): Constitution.

Glass and Allied Workers' Union: Report on the strike at Armourplate Safety Glass - The first legal strike by African Workers in South Africa, South African Labour Bulletin, 3, 7, 1977.

Haarløv/Schmidt: Den Politiske udvikling i Sydafrika i 1970'erne med saerlig vaegt på forholdene på det sorte arbejdsmarked, København, 1979.

Hemson, D.: Trade Unionism and the Struggle for Liberation in South Africa, Capital & Class, 6, 1978.

Hemson, D.: Liberation and Working Class Struggles in South Africa, Review of African Political Economy, 9, 1978.

Herbstein, Dennis: White Man We Want To Talk To You, London, 1978.

Horner, D.: African Labour Representation and the Draft Bill to Amend the Bantu Labour Relations Regulations Act (no. 48, 1953), South African Labour Bulletin, 9, 10, 1976.

Horner, D.: The Western Province Workers Advice Bureau, South African Labour Bulletin, 3, 2, 1976.

Horner, D. (ed.): Labour Organization and the African Worker, SAIRR, Johannesburg, 1975.

Horrell, M.: South African Trade Unionism, SAIRR, Johannesburg, 1961.

Horrell, M.: South African's Workers. Their Organizations and the Patterns of Employment, SAIRR, Johannesburg, 1969.

Hyman, R.: Strikes, Fontana/Colling, Glasgow, 1977.

Hyman, R.: Marxism and the Sociology of Trade Unionism, Pluto Press, 1975.

Ibsen/Jørgensen: Fagbevaegelse og Stat, Aalborg, 1978.

The Institute for Industrial Education: The Workers Handbook no.1., A History of Worker Organizations, Durban, 1977.

The Institute for Industrial Education: The Durban Strikes 1973. Durban, 1976.

ISSA: Südafrika: Schwarze Arbeiter organisieren sich, Von Einem Korrespondenten, ISSA Informationsstelle südliches Afrika, Bonn, August 1976.

Kane-Berman, J.: The Method in the Madness, London, 1978.

Lacey, Marian: Working for Boroko. The origin of a coercive Labour System in South Africa, Johannesburg, 1981.

Legassick, M.: Gold, agriculture and secondary industry in South Africa, 1885-1970: From periphery to sub-metropole, mimeo, n.d.

Legassick, M.: Postscript to "Legislation, Ideology and Economy in post-1948 South Africa", In Schlemmer/Webster (ed.): Change, Reform and Economic Growth in South Africa, Johannesburg, 1978.

Legassick/Hemson: Crisis, the State and Working Class Strategies in South Africa, mimeo, CSE, Bradford, 1978.

Leistner/Breytenback: The Black Worker of South Africa, Pretoria, 1975.

Lewsen, J.: The Role of Registered Unions in the Black Trade Union Movement, South African Labour Bulletin, 3, 4, 1977.

Lewis, D.: African Trade Unions and the South African State: 1947-53, mimeo, Cape Town, 1976.

Lenin, V.I.: What is to be done?, Selected Works, Moscow, 1976.

Lipset/Throw/Colemann: Union Democracy, New York, 1956.
Loft, Mark: Interview with Alec Erwin (tape) 1980.

Luckhardt/Wall: Organize ... or Starve! The History of SACTU, London, 1980.

Luxemburg, Rosa: The Mass Strike, Ceylon, 1970.

Mafeje, A.: Soweto and its Aftermath. Review of African Political Economy, 11, 1979.

Magubane, Bernard Makhosezwe: The Political Economy of Race & Class in South Africa, Monthly Review Press, 1979, New York & London.

Mandel, E.: Leninistisk organisationsteori og proletarisk klassebevidsthed, Fjerritslev, 1972.

Maree, J.: The Dimensions and Causes of Unemployment and underemployment in South Africa, South African Labour Bulletin, 4, 4, 1978.

Merwe, P.J. van der: Unemployment in South Africa. South African Labour Bulletin, 4, 4, 1978.

Michels, R.: Political Parties, New York, 1954.

Morris, M.: Apartheid, Agriculture and the State The Farm Labour Question, Saldru Working Paper no. 8, Cape Town, July 1977.

Mvubelo, Lucy: (Ed. B. Blamick) A Black Trade Union Leader Looks at the Role of American Companies in South Africa, California Institute of Technology, 1980. Munger Africana Library Notes.

Mvubelo, Lucy: (Interview with) National Union of Clothing Workers, South African Labour Bulletin, 5, 3, 1979.

Olsen/Tetzschner: Til skaerm i vor nød, Materialistisk organisationsteori, København, 1979.

Olsen/Tetzschner: Organisationsstruktur og aendringer i fagbevaegelsen - Teori, mimeo, Copenhagen, 1978.

O'Meara, Dan: Analysing Afrikaner Nationalism: The "Christian-National" Assault on White Trade Unionism in South Africa,1934-48, African Affairs, vol. 77, no. 306, jan. 1978.

Poulantzas, N.: Diktaturernas fall: Portugal Grekland och Spanien, Zenit, nr. 47, 19/6.

Redaktionskollektiv Gewerkschaften: Betingelser for socialistisk fagforeningsarbejde, Kurasje, 11, 1975.

Rok, Ajulu; Wiehahn and Riekert: New Mechanism for Control and Oppression of Black Labour and Trade Unions, The Institute of Labour Studies, Discussion Paper, Maseru, Lesotho, 1981.

South African Congress of Trade Unions (SACTU):
Background to apartheid, trade unionism. 1978.
Economic crisis in South Africa, workers burden, 1978.
Workers in chains, 1976.
Mine workers' Conditions, 1976.
Workers Struggle for Freedom, 1976.
Looking Forward, 1977.
Memoranda to the ILO, 1979 & 1980.

Sandbrook, R.: Proletarians and African Capitalism, The Kenyan Case 1962-72, Cambridge, 1975.

Schlemmer/Webster (ed.): Change, Reform and economic growth in South Africa, Johannesburg, 1978.

Simkins/Desmond (ed.): South Africa Unemployment: A Black Picture, Pietermaritzburg, 1978.

Simson, H.: The Social Origins of Afrikaner Fascism and its Apartheid Policy, Uppsala, 1980.

South African Allied Workers' Union (SAAWU): Constitution.

South African Institute of Race Relations: A Survey of Race Relations in South Africa 1976, 1979 & 1980.

South African Pressclips: 1) Agriculture and Farm Labour in South Africa. 2) Opposition to Republic Day. 3) Women in South Africa. Produced by Perry Streek, P.O. Box 84 Houthbay, 7872, South Africa.

Stares, Rodney: Black Trade Unions in South Africa. The responsibilities of British Companies, Christian Concern for Southern Africa, London, 1977.

Sullivan, Leon: The Role of Multinational Corporations in South Africa, SAIRR, Johannesburg, 1981.

Sunesson, S.: Politik och Organisation. Staten och Arbetarklassens Organisationer, Stockholm, 1974.

Toit, du D.: Capital & Labour - Class Struggles in the 1970's, Holland, 1981.

Tostensen, Arne: "Fagorganisering & Arbeidsmarkedsregulering i Sør-afrika". Internasjonal Politik, Nr. 3B supplement 1980.

Urban Training Project (UTP):
Shop Steward Manual.
Notes on Victimisation.
Negotiation Course.
Memorandum on the Bantu Labour Relations Regulations Amendment Act.
Report 1975.
Report 1976, Johannesburg.

Webster, Eddie (ed.): Essays in Southern African Labour History. Ravan Press, Johannesburg, 1978.

Webster/Kuzwayo: A Research Note on Consciousness and the Problem of Organization, in Schlemmer/Webster (ed.): Change, Reform and Economic Growth in South Africa. Johannesburg 1978.

(Western Province) General Workers Union, Submission to the Department of Manpower with Regard to the Proposed Industrial Conciliation Amendment Bill, April 1981.

Wiehahn Commission: Report of the Commission of Inquiry into Labour Legislation, Pretoria, 1979.

Wolpe, H.: The Changing Class Structure of South Africa: The African Petit-bourgeoisie, mimeo, University of Essex, Nov. 1976.